Salisbury. Garden in the Close

GEOFFREY JELLICOE

The Studies of a Landscape Designer over 80 Years

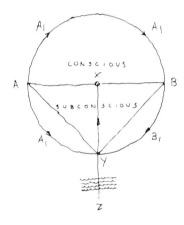

VOLUME II

Gardens & Design
Gardens of Europe

GARDEN · ART · PRESS

British Library Cataloguing-in-Publication Data
A catalogue record for this book is available from the British Library

Published by Garden Art Press
a division of Antique Collectors' Club

Printed in England on Consort Royal Satin paper from Donside Mills, Aberdeen,
by the Antique Collectors' Club Ltd., Woodbridge, Suffolk IP12 1DS

THE STUDIES OF A
LANDSCAPE DESIGNER

This four-volume collection of writings comprehend some seventy years of the practice, experience and philosophy of landscape design. They describe how the concept of an active subconscious is emerging to help organise and give meaning to the making of the modern environment. The Greek philosopher Heraclitus (500 B.C.) wrote: 'The unconscious harmonises the conscious'.

The Studies are in four volumes:

Volume I: *Soundings,* being an introductory personal tour through conscious and subconscious time

An Italian Study, being a critical study of the original drawings in *Italian Gardens of the Renaissance*

Baroque Gardens of Austria

Volume II: *Gardens and Design* and *Gardens of Europe;* pre-war studies, critical and creative

Volume III: *Studies in Landscape Design,* where the concept of the subconscious emerges

Volume IV: *The Guelph Lectures on Landscape Design, Instinct and Mind* and *Jung and the Art of Landscape*

CONTENTS: VOLUME II

GARDENS & DESIGN

J.C. SHEPHERD A.R.I.B.A.
and
G.A. JELLICOE A.R.I.B.A.

First published 1927 by Ernest Benn Limited

"I went into a house, and it wasn't a house.
It has big steps and a great big hall;
But it hasn't got a garden,
A garden,
A garden,
It isn't like a house at all."

When We Were Very Young, A. A. Milne

CONTENTS: GARDENS & DESIGN

ACKNOWLEDGEMENT

In the preparation of these sketches on Garden Design we have to acknowledge the kindness of those without whose help and advice they would have been impossible. For permission to visit the various gardens illustrated in Part I we wish particularly to thank Mr. and Mrs. Berens (Kevington), Mr. Herbert Johnson (Marshcourt), the Rt. Hon. Douglas Tennant (Great Maytham), Mr. and Mrs. C.E. Hughes (The Priory, Orpington), and the Rt. Hon. Lord Waring (Foots Cray Place); also Mr. Inigo Thomas for the photo of the Villa Lante, Mr. B. Cumine for that of the Villa Dona Dalle Rosa, Mr. J.A. Jellicoe for that of the garden at Lahore, Miss Stanley for procuring photos of the Nishat Bagh and the Shalimar, and Messrs. R.B. Holmes and Company, Peshawar, for permission to reproduce them; the Hon. H.D. McLaren for permission to reproduce the Paradise Carpet, Mr. Percy B. Tubbs for the loan of the print of the Villa d'Este, and Mr. L.H. Bucknell, Mr. P.D. Hepworth, and Mr. Oliver Hill for the loan of plans and drawings; lastly, Messrs C.A. Mees, Santpoort, Holland, for permission to reproduce drawings of designs by Frank Lloyd Wright, and to Mr. F. Mansell for the photo of Mondragone.

Under Part II we must thank all in Italy and France for consistent kindness and courtesy, and particularly M. Sommier for permission to visit Vaux-le-Vicomte, and to Madame Vallée of the Calcography department of the Louvre. For The English Tradition we are especially indebted to those without whose permission it would have been impossible to complete a sequence of gardens; namely, to Mr. Norman Jewson (Owlpen Manor), the late Mrs. Boswell Smith (Bingham's Melcombe); Mr. Baron Ash (Packwood House), Sir Arthur Dryden, Bart. (Canons Ashby), Col. Lane Fox (Bramham Park), Mr. Herbert Elliot, for the Duke of Buccleugh (Boughton House), and Mr. Colchester-Wemyss (Westbury-on-Severn). In this part we must thank Miss B. Scott for the photo of the Villa Gamberaia, and Les Archives Photographiques d'Art et d'Histoire for permission to reproduce that of Chantilly.

Under Part III we have to thank Mr. Aggs particularly for permission to visit Little Thakeham.

Lastly, we must refer to the generosity of Mr. F.R. Yerbury in allowing us the choice of his wide collection of photographs; to Messrs. A. Percival for their admirable developing and printing of photographs; and to Mr. C.E. Hughes, on behalf of the publishers, whose interest and knowledge of the subject have been of real value in the production.

J.C.S.
G.A.J.
London, September 1927

1994 FOREWORD

Soon after *Italian Gardens of the Renaissance* had been published in 1925 by Ernest Benn Ltd., a director of the firm, C.E. Hughes, proposed that we should write a book on garden design generally. We gathered at Hughes' lovely home, The Priory, Orpington, Kent, for the first of many discussions. Hughes (it was always surnames) had two passions: early English watercolours, on which he was an authority with a fine collection himself, and gardens. (In later years he made a superb model of the Villa Gamberaia, which with ourselves he regarded as the greatest garden of all time.)

Strange through it may seem today when books on the subject proliferate, the concept was new and simple: to establish garden design as an art rather than as an appendage to horticulture. It was clearly an attempt, too, to rationalise the conflicting ideas of those garden protagonists at the turn of the century, William Robinson and Reginald Blomfield. Of contemporary influences the author most admired the partnership of Edwin Lutyens and Gertrude Jekyll. The main influence, however, was unquestionably Geoffrey Scotts' *Architecture of Humanism* whose 'fallacies' exposed the shallowness of contemporary architecture and thought.

Gardens and Design was well received on publication. It was sound, solid, classic-romantic and essentially British, and it was undoubtedly the foundation from which rose the works described in *The Guelph Lectures on Landscape Design* some sixty years later.

Geoffrey Jellicoe
Highpoint 1995

PART 1

I

PEOPLE AND GARDENS

That caprice, the garden, imprints upon the countryside all the lights and shadows of humanity. Although it is a place of pleasant relaxation, the whole significance is founded on reason. It is from reason that it comes into being at all, and it is reason that has coloured every beautiful plan. We know that while the garden throws over us a spell, the spell is intimately founded on common sense. Reason gives the design, and round design are woven all those fanciful fantastic ideas that are figments of the human brain, things that are mostly illusion.

The planning of the garden is as much a matter of logic as that of the house. The nature of soil, aspect, and any material interests already on the site, all have their influence on the design. If privacy is important, logic suggests the entrance front of the house is so placed to shield the garden behind; and if sun is wanted in the rooms facing the garden, it follows the approach is from the north. In the disposition of the garden, the parts fall naturally into their relative positions round the house; and are as accessible as possible. Immediately round the living-rooms are gathered all that is purely for pleasure and beauty, flowers and lawns. Because flowers prefer protection, it is logical to plant them in enclosed places or back them by a wall or hedge; lawns enjoy winds and open spaces. It is logical to conform to the lie of the land: if it falls, to make terraces that are easy to walk upon; if it is flat, to break up the ground into compartments by evergreens or walls, that stop the winds and give the same protection as the terraces. Paths and walks have a purpose, to lead somewhere by the most reasonably direct route, generally a straight line. There are steps for human beings, but ramps for barrows. Shade is necessary in the summer, and a shaded garden is as important near the house as elsewhere. It is logical to grow climbing roses over pergolas to provide shade, because in winter the roses lose their leaves and nothing but the structure remains to keep out the winter sun. If hot-houses are essential for planting out, there is no reason why, like the old orangeries, they should not adjoin and be a feature of their flower garden, being well designed in themselves. Everything has a purpose, and something that has been misplaced resents it always.

The charm of a garden lies in its power over the human being, to lure him away from the cares of the world into a land of perpetual present. A garden is not wholly for pleasure, for it refreshes; and to this end the arts play upon the emotions. Perhaps the greatest secret lies in the intimacy and peacefulness of the communion with nature. Trees and flowers and plants are here in supreme repose, as though in a haven from the outside world. They offer a welcome excluded to none. Here come birds to play or wash or search for worms. The air is humming with the insect world, and there is life in the quiver of a leaf. Every sense is drawn as if by a magnet into the affairs around: underfoot is the free elastic feel of turf; and over all the sweet scent of nature casts a spell at times recalling the past fleeter than

Villa d'Este, Lake Como. Stillness deepened by dripping fountains

memory itself. Association plays its own strange rôle. There is that which peoples the emptiest garden with personal memories or the romance of history; and that which gives ideas of other things by things seen. A shape, a sound, a colour, suggests something to the imagination. Flowers are lively, animate, little things: tiger lilies are in violent conversation, pansies are confiding, lupins rear themselves proudly and indifferently. A willow tree is weeping although as contented as its neighbour. The cypress towering above the theatre in the garden at Siena reminds us by its own eternity how quickly the actors pass across the stage. So every flower and plant, shrub or tree, in nature, suggests an emotion. Architecture expresses these things in a similar way. Long simple lines, recalling cadences of prose and poem, are calm and stately; broken lines are more excited. Steps and stairways are in perpetual motion, flowing up or pouring down; they can be sombre, or

Villa Gori, Siena. Association of ideas: perpetuity and change in the theatre

laughing, or bored to the point of yawning. Over all reigns the house, kindly
or forbidding. Sounds also are full of meaning, often giving voice to their
natural surroundings. A landscape is rendered more impressive, more vital,
if it gives forth a note like the cry of an animal. Seagulls tell of the wild
spaces of the sea, the lowing of cattle of calm and peaceful fields: a garden
speaks through water and the infinite notes of birds. Association, too, leads
to invitation: a seat, a glimpse of sunlight and green seen through a
doorway in a town house, or shade on a hot summer's day. It is by
suggestion that colour warms or cools almost as well as do sun and shade in
fact. In Italy the colour is the subtlest shades of evergreens and stone, and
under the strong sun is restful and refreshing. In England the bright colour
of flowers and warm red brick enlivens an atmosphere that is generally too
sombre. The gorgeousness of the tropics, where flowers and costumes flash

Nishat Bagh, Kashmir.
Landscape dominating

Mondragone, Frascati.
Landscape dominated

Cleeve Prior Manor, Evesham. Mystery of an enclosed approach

Villa near Florence. Landscape perfectly attuned

back the rays of the sun, is too high-pitched for northern eyes. Perhaps it is through association that sculpture makes its first appeal in the garden, for it sums up the spirit of everything there, and interprets it to human understanding. The material and lasting influence of these associations is probably in no case so considerable as that of natural landscape. The constant presence of a landscape can often mould a man's whole outlook, just as in the course of time it has moulded whole races. There is a sense of the sublime about mountains and peaks that soar into the air thunderous and oppressive, for the gods live there and must not be disturbed. Open plains mean prosperity and peace, and are reassuring. A view over the weald of Sussex of villages, farms, fields, cattle, scattered trees, and woods, is light and playful and transitory; a view over the rolling downs beyond is ever-lasting. In time sublimity, repose, delight or constancy finds the soul of the man who lives in its presence.

These intimate feelings and associations, while they may vary slightly with each person, are more or less common to all. They are the atoms that go to make the garden before design steps in, and are unchanging. But the human mind is essentially changeful. No two minds are alike, and this finds its expression in the disposition and type. A personality that is broad and of even temperament may be content with a place of pure simplicity, provided it is well proportioned; on the other hand, one that is temperamental feels at home only in excessive variety. People who are themselves of definite character respond to definite gardens; and the Far East, for instance, have even provided those that are martial or religious. Again, every part of the garden finds its mysterious echo in the human mind. To one person an approach to his house through towering cliffs of

Grand Trianon, Versailles. Vitality and repose

yew may be dark and foreboding, in another it may awaken a chord of sympathy and invitation; to both it is a preparation for what is to come. A tired mind responds to the quiet simple lines of an enclosed lawn, where a view by its constantly changing interests would be too stimulating. For this reason a garden composed of view alone becomes to most people oppressive; in all respects the mind can absorb only a certain amount of interest. In England the garden contains the interest of flowers, and the form has always remained simple probably for this reason. In Italy, where climate precludes flowers, the interest lies in the form, which is keyed from the pattern of box parterre to the rich shapes of the scheme itself. While the personality of a man may thus fit in with his own garden, so that he and nature are at home together, he cannot himself fit in visibly. The mind can shed the needs of society and civilisation as he wanders away among the trees and flowers, but the body cannot. That is why the presence of a second person often destroys the spell of the wilder parts of the garden.

The first of the sensations to cast a spell is repose. Only on a foundation of repose can there be built the variety that makes the garden stimulating. Repose depends mainly on unity, where everything is ruled over by an all-presiding genius. Symmetry is restful, both because the simple balance of the parts does not require any effort to be appreciated, and because the eye easily finds its resting-place. If symmetry becomes too insistent, it no longer

Great Maytham, Kent. (By Sir Edwin Lutyens.) The view, showing simplicity of foreground

Great Maytham, Kent. The flower garden, showing simplicity of background

gives repose so much as restraint to the imagination. Straight lines are more restful than broken lines or curves, and a calm silhouette to the garden may quell all the flowers that are bursting with vitality inside. An enemy to repose is divided attention, for it can ruin the grandest view or the smallest detail. If the garden embraces the country the climax is either on the garden itself or on the country. If the latter is rich and full of interest, the former is simple and any interests that might distract are put out of sight. Similarly, a rich piece of ironwork may be a perfect entry to a lawn or a gravel walk, but a perpetual source of irritation to a flower garden. While a fine sensation can be so lightly ruined, it can be heightened by contrast. Contrast is the energy of design. The clematis that clings to the house emphasises the strength of architecture, and revels in its own fragility. Stillness is deepened by a murmur; the shade of an alley by the dappled patches of sun that penetrate the branches and suggest the heat outside. The intimacy of an enclosed garden emphasises the breadth of the open view. Square shapes foil a circle. The greatest contrast of all is to leave the sombre house and step into space and sunlight. Concentration of effect is equally magical, for a group of simple daisies may seem rich where many richer flowers, spread over a wider area, would nullify themselves and appear commonplace. Contrasts over-stressed become abrupt and jarring. There is between contrasts some elusive bond of sympathy; small elements of the one are introduced into the other. The most violent contrast of all lies always between house and country, art and nature, and there is between the two a constant interchange of sympathy. Contrast leads to interest. The more a garden is divided into parts that are secluded one from another, the more interesting does it become. There is the element of surprise, which perpetually deceives. The garden is not wholly seen at once; there are places full of mystery. In the depths of our own orchard, with the branches interlacing overhead in fairy patterns, we can disagree with Keats that fancy never stayed at home. Other places are kept away because they are conceits, and conceits wear thin with constant use. One person may enjoy a grotto where secret fountains spring upon the unwary guest; another prefers his rock garden, where strange and beautiful plants are staged profusely. The little theatre in the garden at Marlia is an idea of peculiar charm, with its wings and prompter's box and footlights clipped in box. These are often the incidents of the garden, phantasies of the moment that have no lasting value. With surprise is coupled wonder, a sudden spectacle seen from a pre-arranged position: a distant view, a mass of flowers, water, a noble avenue of trees. Provided it is not sustained, but is come and gone in a flash, the mind, even though experiencing it from day to day, receives a refreshing and stirring stimulus. Drama in any form takes a sudden but purely passing hold of the imagination. There is the pleasure, too, of showing the garden to newcomers. Over visitors, if their stay is short, the spell of the garden cannot easily be thrown, and the touch of drama given by a sequence of sensations is invaluable.

A source of intimacy between man and his garden is scale. Scale is the sense of size that each person associates with the various parts. In certain respects it is fixed, for, like steps, some parts are similar for all humans. Such

Villa Marlia, Lucca. Fantasy

a size as the width of a grass walk is settled only by personal feeling for space. To one person it may appear narrow; to another it is in perfect tune, and is materialistic and comfortable; to a third, it may appear above human scale and create a suggestion of the sublime. The breadth of a man's mind is implanted in the scale of his garden. But scale again is elusive; mere size is crude. Our walk may become so wide as to appear bare; at once it loses its significance, and what was before a shape suggesting a fine movement is now a space without a meaning. It is unity that pitches the scale. Size and scale have little in common, because a great area may be divided up into a number of small parts, and thus be smaller in scale than a place half its size that has not been divided. The appreciation of size is given by scale: the eye seizes upon a detail, and leaps from this stage by stage to the main idea. The movement is instantaneous, but any stage that is out of scale tends to interfere with its course. A thing in itself has no size to the human eye unless seen in relation to something whose size is definitely known. In nature, a leaf gives the size of the branch that gives the size of the tree. Steps give the size of a flight, that gives the size of a walk, that in turn suggests the size of the scheme.

To a certain extent it follows that the larger the scheme, the higher is the scale pitched, because a greater undertaking is associated with greater ideas. In these larger schemes that are beyond the grasp of one man, there appears a garden that is no longer individual, but collective. This is the entertaining garden, a garden for other people. People are the very essence of its existence. It sweeps away the finer shades of feeling, to represent the feelings of the mass. So strong has been the sensation in gardens designed

Marly-le-Roi

At Lahore

solely for entertaining, that where in its quieter moments it is a private garden, the owner has found it necessary to make a small personal garden entirely detached from the main scheme. In Italy this small garden was known as the 'giardino secreto', and is found in practically every garden laid out in the grand manner. The entertaining garden depends upon constant movement and the intercourse of people. It is a magnificent foil to people magnificently dressed. It is the drama of an afternoon or night, and in the passing hours are crammed pleasures of the moment. Great spaces cry aloud for people. Clipped walls of evergreens keep themselves dark and simple. Giant gatepiers, bristling at their tops, herald the passage of people in between. Lines of terraces one above the other provide walks for the throng to move backwards and forwards, looking down upon the extent of people below, or to be seen themselves by those below in tier upon tier. Ramps and stairs intermingle persons one with another, emphasising their movements with their own. Flowers creep away from the main garden, ousted from their position by the spectacle of people. Just as flowers in smaller gardens have been carefully chosen for their position, so are people unified with the architecture. Costumes intermix and play together, and throw up their colours in a constantly changing kaleidoscope. While the main scheme stretches with people gossiping, joking, laughing, so in the parts round about are interests to amuse when they grow weary of conversation. There is a maze where they can lose themselves, a theatre, water gardens, grottoes, and all sorts of other surprises. At Marly Louis XIV built himself such a pleasure garden when he tired of Versailles and the Trianon. The position is a huge natural amphitheatre of the hills, looking out across the winding Seine to the blue hills beyond. In the centre was the King's own house, and on either side stretched six small guest-houses connected by pleached alleys. Behind these were woods that contained all manner of woodland glades and gardens. In front of them terrace upon terrace led down to where a sheet of water lay shimmering under the sky. This beautiful place, resting so luxuriously in the lap of the hills, was ideal to hold the graceful pompous courtiers of the time.

These great gardens carry us out of ourselves to see in the gardens of other lands the character and habits of a nation. In Versailles and Marly there is no personal individuality, no intimate communion between man and nature. The gardens reflect only the glory of the French nation; every weakness is hidden behind a veil of artificiality. In Italy it was different. At the time of the Renaissance individualism was strong enough to break up the country into separate states. A garden was a personal necessity of each man, reflecting the many sides of his character; and so it is that Italy has that amazing variety of types each of which is a constant reminder of her intellectualism. European art tells of races that are intensely alive and progressive, where every moment is a step won or lost in civilisation, the south studied and calculating, the north more lyrical. When we cross the Pyrenees into Spain, we find in the patios and Moorish gardens the mysticism that bears us across the seas to the gardens of India and Kashmir. Here were people wrapped in the mystery of life. For generations they remained unchanged, looking upon life as one long rhythm of time. For them the garden played the largest part in their national art and life; it was a symbol of God, of Life and Eternity. Gardens were laid out from the description of Paradise in the Koran, in eight parts or terraces; every tree and flower having its meaning. Their gardens remained simple because they never strove to penetrate beyond what already satisfied them. Colour, flowers, scent, and above all association, must cast over the senses a spell that is hypnotic. It is the beginning of studied emotions, and the proportion of those of repose to those of stimulation is overwhelming. The East can carry us back through the ages in mighty strides. In time we shall come to that first garden, where the problem of art and nature did not exist.

II

ART AND NATURE

We feel but cannot understand the mysteries of nature around. Sunshine, fleecy clouds scudding across the sky, country of every variety and type, trees and foliage that never repeat themselves, forests and hills, colour that passes through the whole range of the spectrum, fields and hedgerows of wild flowers, water in its myriad forms, birds and wild fowl with a colouring as subtle as it is brilliant. Today all this is beyond us, though once man stepped straight into it from his cave. Now the world is no longer our garden, and we have to make round ourselves an art in sympathy with the artificiality of our existence. For this we draw upon what lies around, and alter it at will. Music is the captured sounds of the earth, and architecture an echo of its forms, but they are far removed from their origin. All that a man stands for is expressed in his building. It is the reflection of his personality and its place in civilisation, and has character of its own. Set it crudely in the midst of country, and trouble arises; it is incongruous. When architecture meets country, and there is peace, some hidden bond of sympathy lies between them. The low, massive Egyptian

Villa Crivelli, near Milan. Widely spaced pylons and statuary concentrating interest and carrying formality into the distance

Ven House, Somerset. Bold introduction between architecture and nature

temples are related to the long bands of sand-dunes among which they rest. The mediaeval castle rises sheer and forbidding from its surroundings, a second rock to the one on which it stands. A sailing ship joins clouds and sea by its sails and shapely bulk. These are abstract relations only, but it is certain that into every building that stands alone with any quality of permanency, nature has crept in a hundred different ways. The supreme example of character and contrast in garden work is fairly represented by the palace of Versailles, and the humblest by the peasant's cottage that nestles under a thatched roof. The one is more pronounced than the other, but the relation to nature is the same in principle. The formal house extends to meet its wild surroundings, and the two discuss their differences in the garden. If the one can surprise by coming to the very door of the house, the other can retaliate by penetrating softly into the sacred precincts round about. The garden that is cut off from its immediate surroundings with high walls and levels, and cannot associate with them, may be equally in harmony with its setting. From without it can settle into its surroundings by grouping and composition. From within it can leap the foreground and mingle with the view, as the more intimate garden with the neighbouring trees.

Let us first consider how the house extends to meet nature. Many a square block has settled comfortably into the country by spreading diminishing waves of formality. The garden grows less formal as it recedes from the house, finally to disappear imperceptibly. Straight lines are broken and

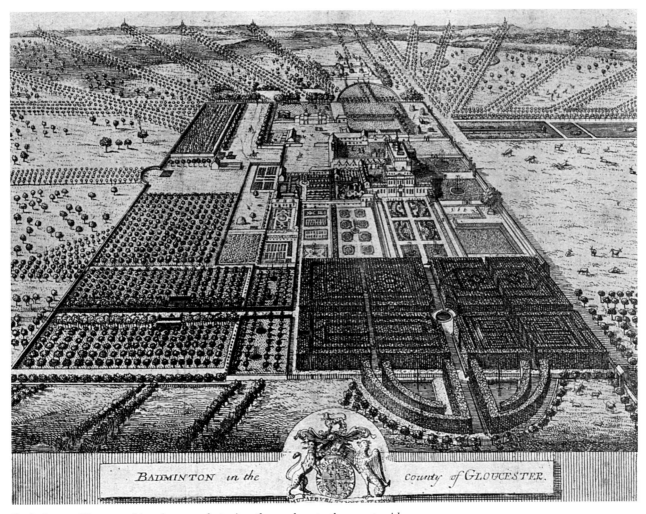

Badminton, Gloucestershire. Avenues fastening the gardens to the countryside

become merely suggested. Lawns and terraces that are as rigid as the rooms they embrace run away into the speckled shadows of trees or the open fields. Paths become less neat. Walks and steps lose their sophistication. Prim beds of flowers give way to flowers running riotously free. Everywhere the dignity of architecture is abandoned. If the extremities of the garden become naturalistic too quickly, the house plants outposts of formality to maintain its presence, breakwaters round which floods the country. It is one of the functions of sculpture to spread the house through the garden. Although in isolated places sculpture expresses the poetry of nature, its material and artificiality give the hint that after all a building is at hand. The avenues and vistas that extend from a house spread its formality over a wider area. The avenues of Badminton radiated from the house and fastened it somewhat crudely to half a county. More sympathetic is the vista that is maintained by clumps of trees or undergrowth. These clumps grow less formal as they recede, and in the far distance merge into the landscape. At Sutton Place the yews advance down the central walk, and on either side the wild grass sweeps up to meet the smooth. A definite scheme of architectural features placed along the avenues punctuates the distances and lends formality and interest. A vista may be suggested simply by opening a way through reasonably wooded country. In Italy widely spaced

Sutton Place, Surrey. Subtle introduction between architecture and nature

twin cypresses are planted, that carry the eye over an unlimited distance of otherwise natural country. In a garden there is nothing so inviting as a walk that runs out into the view, missing the middle distance, for it leads the eye far away from its immediate surroundings. On the other hand, it is possible to consider a house and garden emerging from, rather than into, their surroundings. Nature is the direct source of inspiration, and from its depths the garden comes bubbling forth, takes itself more seriously as it approaches, grows dignified, and at last merges into the full stateliness of architecture. Only on rare occasions is such a conception possible. The gardens at La Granja in Spain come out of the hills, while at the Villa Lante in Italy the wooded slopes conspire to send down to the town of Bagnaia a garden that is possibly the finest in the country.

To entice the countryside into the garden requires more subtlety, and perhaps the first need is for a garden set openly to reflect the scale and character of its surroundings. The gardens at Frascati are view-gardens overlooking the sweep of the Roman Campagna, and they have absorbed something of its splendour. No view in England has a similar scale, and with the country split up into hedges and trees, meadows and roads, the gardens it contains are smaller and more personal. Country may have a character that cannot be ignored, stamping the garden in its own likeness. The gardens of Japan are set in a land of hills and hillocks, whose character is so dominating that it seems as though plants and architecture swing in unison. The long lines of the hill terraces in Spain and elsewhere that have been made since immemorial times for planting have demanded horizontal lines of any garden in their midst, whether constructionally necessary or not. The chessboard of meadows in an English plain suggests the simple rectangle shapes of the traditional garden. Similarly, parts of a less pronounced country find their counterpart in parts of the garden. The parterre of the terrace at Cuzzano near Verona is shared with the whole valley, and its pattern is a culmination to the endless furrows chasing along

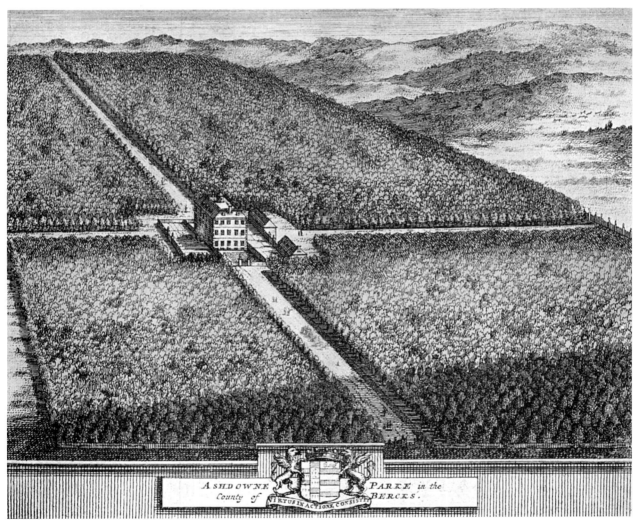

Ashdown Park, Berkshire. House and garden emerging from surroundings

La Granja, Spain. Garden emerging from woods

Villa Lante, Italy. Garden emerging intimately from trees

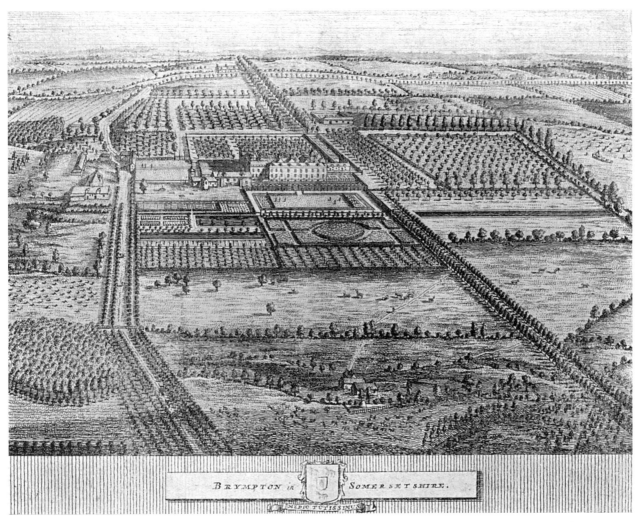

Brympton, Somerset. A traditional English garden settling into a country of meadows

the hillside. The broad sweep of the bowling green at Bingham's Melcombe recalls into the heart of the garden the meadow across the way, over which it is looking. A stretch of water that is not reflecting its immediate surroundings imprisons light and plants upon the ground a portion of the ever-changing sky. Ornament is susceptible to nature and can become the formal embassy of its surroundings. Sculpture in an open plain is broad and distant, exuding the breath of the view. The fountain that stands before the Villa Bernardini in Italy helps to draw into the garden the hills behind with which it contrasts. In a wood sculpture tells of the mystery of trees, echoing their lines in its own. The nymph floating on the water in the garden near Stockholm mates with water-lilies. Intimate decoration reflects the flowers and foliage beside it, planting upon the surface of buildings what has already been planted in the garden. Baroque artists in Italy penetrated into this spirit of nature and interpreted it frankly in their work. Their love of movement and drama led them specially to seek out the emotions of water. They seized upon its gaiety and held it in the laughing curves of fountains. They perpetuated the ripples for ever playing across the lakes in the steps and stairways that link their gardens to the water. They built the long terraces that belong, not to the hills and mountains from which they are

Villa Bernardini, Lucca. Sympathy of sculpture to distant natural surroundings

hewn, but to the flatness of water from which they rise. The island of Isola Bella, with its tier upon tier of terraces, floats for ever upon the surface of Lake Maggiore. These are more or less things of the imagination, but the country is more clearly a part of the garden when its own materials are used, the living trees and shrubs and plants, local bricks and stone, and water. Water slips into the garden fresh from nature, varies its mood at will from light frivolity to utter gloom, and slips out again as brisk and bright as ever. It is the most versatile of all materials. It disappears and reappears, and in a moment its clamour has become the song of the garden, and its

Garden of Carl Milles, Stockholm. Relation of sculpture to intimate natural surroundings

waywardness the countless different forms of pattern. With trees, the slender forms of palms are as much at home among the echoing minarets and flat plains of the East as the firs among the mountain peaks and chalets of Switzerland. Both are at a loss in a healthy English country of rolling downs and rounded trees, where everything is robust and rich and luscious, and where the circumstances that gave their shape no longer exist. Imported specimens need not be as out of place as these. The cypress is generally at home in any garden, not because it reflects nature so much as the formality of architecture. Remove the cypress from a very formal garden setting in England, and it is as much out of place in its own way as a fir. Such rare foreign trees as tulip are magnificent in an English garden, for their shape is both formal and sympathetic to indigenous trees. All trees and plants, whether imported or not, are subject to design as soon as they enter the sphere of the garden. Design composes trees in relation to their formal surroundings and introduces foliage as grouping or as pure pattern over the formal lines of architecture, softening them by colour, light and shade. Formal hedges and lawns are the threshold of the house. Here nature is all the healthier for being in submission, and so the trees enjoy their clipping, and the lawns their mowing and rolling. Clipped hedges with their form are of all living materials probably the most related to the solidity of the house. Their texture is a consideration. While a yew hedge has a great beauty from

Isola Bella, Lago Maggiore. Affinity of terraces to the surface of the water

Boboli Gardens, Florence. Affinity of detail to water

*Fountain in the Courtyard, Fredericksborg Castle, Denmark. Water-spouts arranged in
relation to setting*

varying shades of surface that mark each tree, a privet hedge is so close
grained that in comparison it appears dull. Flowers are very sensitive to
their position. Foreign flowers that need special treatment seem to repel
their surroundings and create round themselves an atmosphere of their
own. The flowers that are most at home are those that once grew wild in the
country round, and have been tended and cared for. The old English rose
is a brother of the brier rose, to which it returns if left unattended.
Honeysuckle can cover the walls more profusely than it grows in the
hedgerows. Similarly flowers and plants are more in place where the soil has
not been specially laid. In very formal gardens some flowers may still be in
character, although foreign. Tulips are from Persia, but, like the cypress
tree, they are beautiful in most gardens because of their formality. While an
herbaceous border is for all comers, flowers in a garden have a strong sense
of social scale. Hydrangeas are so rich and overwhelming that they claim a
magnificent position; they have, in fact, become almost a part of the
architecture. But it is more the solidity of the garden that brings it into
relation with the ground upon which it stands. For this reason the use of
local materials makes the buildings appear as though they too have sprung
from the soil; and the more natural the surface of the material the closer do
they belong. If the country is chalk, the whiteness of chalk stands out clear
and refreshing; and because a chalk quarry has occasional ribs of flint, the
surface of buildings will be softened if some of this is introduced as pattern.

Above: Little Bognor, Sussex (By C. Williams-Ellis)
Below: Cicogna, North Italy
Relation through a similar character of free-growing planting to architecture

Marshcourt, Hampshire. Hedges carrying on the solidity of architecture

In Northamptonshire the rich yellow stone hewn locally is integral with the countryside, just as by the seaside pebbles recall the shore into the garden. The design of details has a direct bearing on their materials. Stone suggests strength and ruggedness; wood suggests airy shapes of pergolas; bricks emphasise their standard size and make, by simple pattern. Of all the ways we have of inviting nature into the garden, none is so sure as that of time. Time has seriously to be reckoned with in design. When the garden is first completed, it inclines to be empty, for if highly finished at the outset by architectural features, the growth of nature may only create confusion by over-interest. But time casts over all an ever-increasing web of nature that continues to draw the garden together as the years go by.

The garden is closely related in its design to any natural features that are outside its boundaries, but whose presence must always exert some influence. A frame steadies a picture and brings it into relation with its architectural surroundings. Windows of a room do the same to a view outside. In a far wider and more versatile way a garden can pick and choose, and decide upon the portion of the view it wishes to include. Where every prospect pleases it can embrace all; though it soon discovers that the limiting of a view often increases the drama. It can blot out offending parts, or reduce the distance to an object. The windmill seen from the garden at Compton Wynyates, in Warwickshire, has now become the centre of an interesting picture; while at Alington Castle the trees are even more an integral part of the design. In the same way a distant object is brought perceptibly nearer when seen from the end of an enclosed walk that is

Above: Alington Castle, Kent. (By Philip Tilden)
Below: Compton Wynyates, Warwickshire
Introduction into the garden of external natural features

Marshcourt, Hampshire. The walk from the North Terrace: Viewpoint A on plan

pointing towards it. Foreground is the intermediary between oneself and the view, and ways are found to increase the interest and quality of the distance. The frame may simply mean that the middle distance has been cut out and the panorama stretches above a steady foreground line. A pair of oaks carefully placed frame in a view a grove of oaks as efficiently as yews frame a sheet of water. The former is related by unison, the latter by contrast. The frame gains in drama if so placed that there is a contrast of space between itself and the picture. The piers that frame the country near Florence are placed at the end of an avenue of cypresses, the moment before the ground dips away into space (p.21). The frame of any picture should be in every way worthy of its purpose; if it is too small it is a nuisance, and if too great it tends to keep out the view by overpowering and detracting from it. These gate-piers with their slender points give the entire meaning to the hills behind. The wings of a house that so often build round three sides of a courtyard enclose a view that is vigorous enough to need such a frame. If, on the other hand, a view is too overpowering, it is broken up into a number of smaller and constantly changing pictures by detached points. A row of yews, a pergola, or even the stems of trees, answer to this and repeat the idea of the glazing bars of the house by carrying across the enclosing lines of the garden. At Marshcourt, in Hampshire, the house is set on the spur of the hills, with a view to the south across a short valley and to the west along a length of the valley of the Tees. The walk that leads round the house on these two sides handles the view skilfully. The terrace at the extreme north, a viewpoint over the country round, is a bare lawn enclosed by rigid yew hedges about four feet high that cut off the middle distance. From this square, steps descend into a long enclosed vista, at first confined to flowers and architectural interests. Beyond the house the enclosing walls are suddenly omitted, and the ground falls away abruptly, almost precipitously after so much protection, to reveal the view. At the turn of the walk, which is again enclosed, there is a recess in the yew, from which a narrow way leads into an alcove facing south. House, garden, flowers, walks – all are forgotten in this remote little place. Out of this by the same way the walk continues to

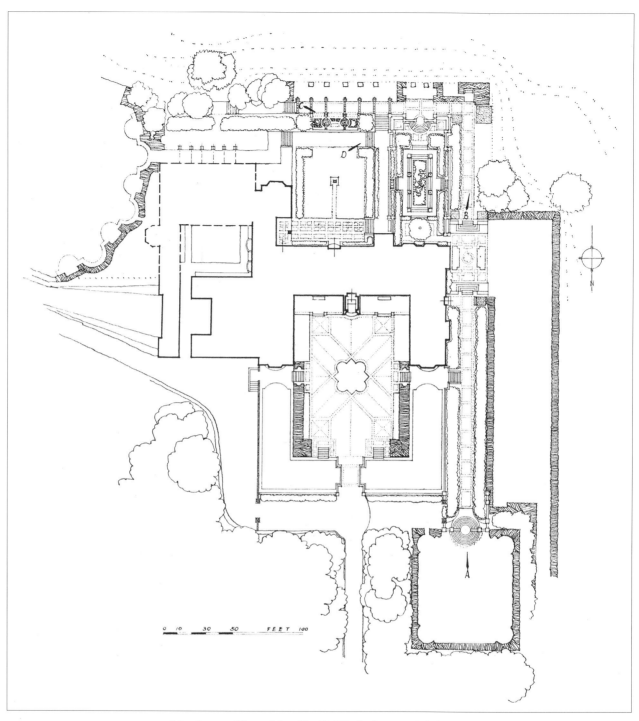

Marshcourt, Hampshire. (By Sir Edwin Lutyens.) A beautifully balanced plan designed for the spur of a hill, the ground falling sharply south and west to a wide view

the east, with occasional glimpses of the view through clipped yew squares, until it reaches the pergola. Through the piers and cross-pieces overhead the view and sky are seen with a comfortable sense of security. The walk then plunges into the darkness of trees, up some steps, and so on to the upper terrace, where garden and view share the open situation.

While there is lateral introduction between the house and surroundings, there is also vertical introduction, the garden considered as a link between

Marshcourt, Hampshire. The opening to the south-west: Viewpoint B on plan

Marshcourt, Hampshire. The Pergola: Viewpoint C on plan

Marshcourt, Hampshire. From the Upper Terrace: Viewpoint D on plan

ground and sky. The sky line is a definite pattern. The dark undersides of trees that soar up and spread out their branches, contrast with the sky itself, for sky, like a view, is appreciated all the more if it is occasionally excluded. Stone pines in the Borghese Gardens at Rome send down shadows from their height, and by giving a sense of protection from above to the seats, open out the arena to the skies. At Kevington, in Kent, and Packwood, in Warwickshire, the elms appearing beyond the walls weave patterns against the sky that give much of the charm to the wall gardens below. The woodland garden of the Grand Trianon at Versailles is a beautiful intermingling of sky and ground. Shadows of passing clouds have a subconscious interest in small gardens, but in places like Versailles or an English park, where a vast area can be seen at once, the shadows that chase across the ground reflect the interest overhead. With all these arts at command to soften the house and its surroundings, there is the chance that sympathy may be overdone. The character of architecture is firmness, and too much planting and broken line may destroy the beautiful contrast that is the vitality of the garden. Flowers at the base of a building may weaken the house where it should be strongest, if the architectural lines that bind it to the ground have been concealed by their profusion. Similarly, too much architecture in the immediate vicinity may nullify its purpose. The firmest base to a house is probably the levelled stretch of lawn that often lies spread before the towers and gables and chimneys of a Tudor or Elizabethan mansion. This straight lawn is already a brother to the undulating meadows around. In the same way the boundaries can suffer from too soft a line between the garden and nature. The ha! ha! was a surprise packet of the

Borghese Gardens, Rome. Umbrella pines breaking up and framing the sky above the Arena

eighteenth century, a sunk ditch across which the garden swept into the country. At Ven House, the point is delicately but firmly marked where the main road passes the entrance gates and separates garden from park. Often the garden loses its character through lack of decision at these points. The balance between ruthlessness and sympathy needs to be very carefully adjusted and must depend upon the circumstances of the moment. If nature at that moment is dull and lifeless, cold and forbidding, then it should be closed out altogether with those same high walls that enclosed

Above: Kevington, Kent
Below: Packwood, Warwickshire
Skyline of trees above a simple enclosed garden

Grand Trianon, Versailles. Intermingling of ground and sky by trees and water

Ven House, Somerset

the monastery gardens of old, when it was death to commune with nature. It must depend upon how each one of us regards country. Probably it is always more pleasant to consider nature smiling, and for us to enjoy it while we can.

III

UNITY

A garden is composed of an incredible variety of elements. Nature alone introduces intricacies that happen in no other art, and flowers and plants and trees, and the subtleties of introduction, easily lead to confusion. The garden, however, is primarily a work of art, and therefore in its initial stages built on pattern. The form of the garden gives the character, and the difficulties may be the inspiration, but the principles of its design are those of any visual pattern. The Persian carpet has little significance other than pure pattern, yet it is practically the design of a Persian garden. From a Persian garden to Le Nôtre is another step in the history of pattern, and from there to the Villa Gamberaia or Marshcourt is still another. It is at this point that the more elastic sister arts leave garden architecture behind, probably because those very intricacies call for a simple basis. However involved the garden may be on the surface, its pattern lies underneath, simple and restful in its unity.

Though theme and rhythm decide the type, disposition, and scale of the design, it is left to balance to turn it into composition. A four-square scheme

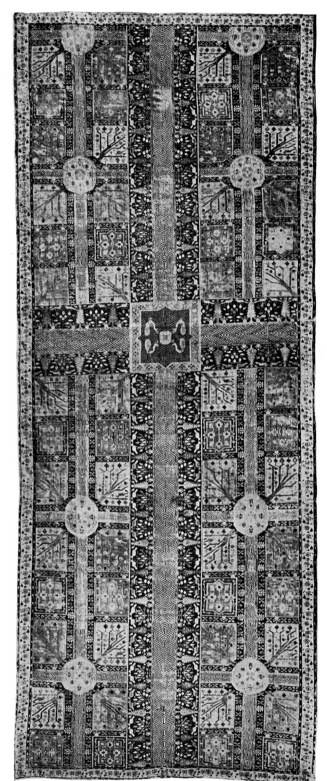

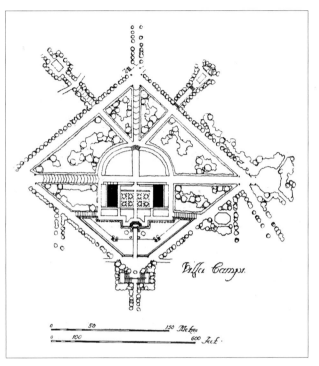

Villa Campi

The Paradise Carpet. Although probably made for Shah Abbas in the seventeenth century, the design goes back at least to Chosroes I, the Sassanian King of Persia (A.D. 531-579). Such gardens as the Shalimar and the Nishat Bagh are concrete examples of the Paradise Garden from which the design is drawn. (See 'Gardens of the Great Mughals', by C. M. Villiers Stuart)

like the Villa Campi, near Florence, turns perpetually on its equal axes, and the focus of interest is in its centre. Similarly, less symmetrical schemes turn about their centres, upon axes that may or may not be stressed. In a picture, line and counter-line wrestle with each other within their allotted limits, neither gaining supremacy. The centre round which they turn is sometimes

Shalimar, Lahore. Expression of the Persian carpet with logical design of watercourses

a focus of interest which draws the eye quicker to its place of rest, and holds it there. Proportion of the parts not only gives life and interest to the whole, but adjusts the balance. A part that is small in shape and rich in interest balances one of a very much larger size that is without interest. Distance from the centre, type, and quality, all have their influence. Parts are proportional one to another in carefully adjusted quantities and shapes, avoiding competition or overmuch contrast, but allowing a little discord to increase the sense of unity. This is the spirit of design, and its relation to the garden is as intimate as to a picture. The parts become spaces, linked together by lines of circulation, and details such as steps, flower-beds, walls, sculpture, conform to make the elements of a vast pattern. The parts that are solid take their positions of importance in the plan. Just as the Shalimar with all its waterways grows from a flat picture similar to the carpet, so the whole scheme merges slowly into the three-dimensional massing of architecture. The pattern of the garden does not necessarily want to be too strong; at once, though the unity of the whole may be perfect, there is a sense of oppression. One of the most elaborate examples in the world is

Villa Dona Dalle Rose, Italy

Versailles, where the Grand Canal hangs like a great jewel from the palace. This main scheme is capable of holding all the variety of elements that happen on either side. A more subtle example from Italy is the Villa Dona Dalle Rosa, at Valzanzibio, where a number of minor interests are held together by two cross axes. The scheme in itself has to be not merely well balanced, but consistent in character. Anything in the way of a 'shape' will be out of place in a cottage garden, which is not sufficiently artificial for so rich a thing as a curve. The character is its ingenuousness. The traditional English garden is square in its idea and character, and even here the introduction of a curve is an event that is very important. On the other hand, French gardens before the eighteenth century were highly artificial, and in every little village round Paris gardens laid out were rich in shape and curves, beside which the English gardens of the same period seem heavy-handed. During the Baroque in Italy, the character of the gardens often depended wholly on curves. In the little eighteenth-century garden of the Arcadian Academy at Rome, the essence of the scheme is a sequence of curves throwing off each other as they proceed upwards. In such a garden a square shape now strikes the important note. Gardens, too, have a definite theme that needs to be followed out. Owlpen Manor is composed of narrow terraces and steep steps reminiscent of mediaeval days, but the garden at Westbury is low and broad and calm, and everything is consistent with the idea of repose.

In itself the elements of a garden could be satisfactorily composed in unlimited different ways, but in reality first the convenience and then the country round narrow the range of composition considerably. Even so, a single garden may be open to many arrangements, from which it is difficult to choose the best. Apart from its significance, the house by its bulk and interest is often the most important part of a garden scheme, and round this the garden balances. Ragly in Warwickshire was a perfect example of exact symmetry, where the entrance approach and side wings were well connected through on either side of the house to the main garden scheme which they balanced. This was a place so neat and correct that, but for the levels, it might have been arranged away from its surroundings. At Stansted,

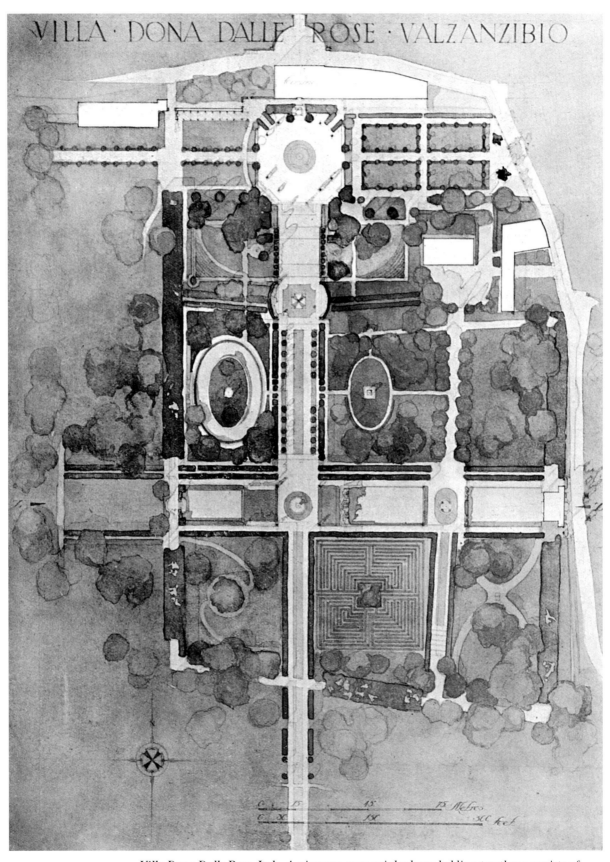

Villa Dona Dalle Rose, Italy. A vigorous cross-axial scheme holding together a variety of interests. Note the contrast and proportioning of the axes in themselves

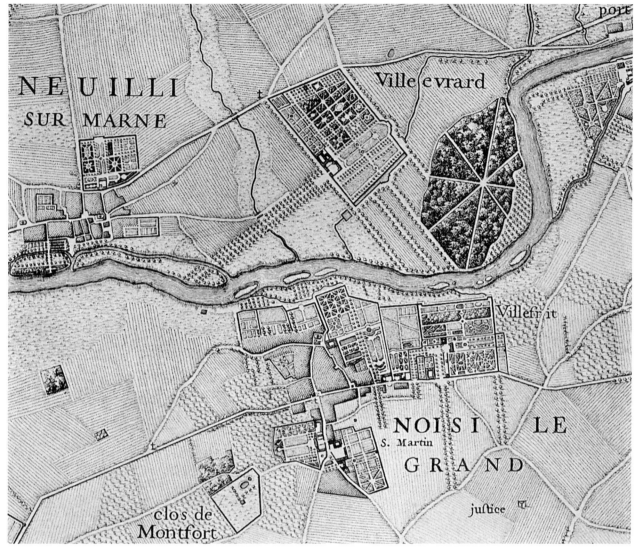

A typical village near Paris, 1740. Illustrating the technique in planning that applied to every small garden. From a Survey by Delagrève

in Sussex, the exact symmetry was eased by the dissimilarity of the church and semicircular garden, and though the parts seem isolated, there is little that could be added or taken away. On the other hand, the garden may have a will of its own, and where it has been boldly flung away from the façade, itself a great open-air room, the scheme is not that of a house standing in its own grounds, but that of a house together with its grounds. They balance about a part that brings them into composition. Whether it is the curved ramps of the Villa d'Este at Tivoli, or the fountain of Latona at Versailles, there is often some part emphasised that knits the two together. Chantilly is a masterpiece of planning. The centre of interest is the statue in the forecourt, and round this swing château, forest, gardens, and canal, in perpetual balance. Just as the garden is the introduction between man and nature, so in a smaller sense it is at times the point of balance of a composition that links the house and the view, the completion of which lies in the imagination. One likes to imagine that the fountain at Mondragone is placed here for that purpose. Again the view can be provided for as an integral part of the composition. In such a garden as Hamstead Marshall,

The Arcadian Academy, 'Il Paradiso', Rome. Consistency of curved shapes

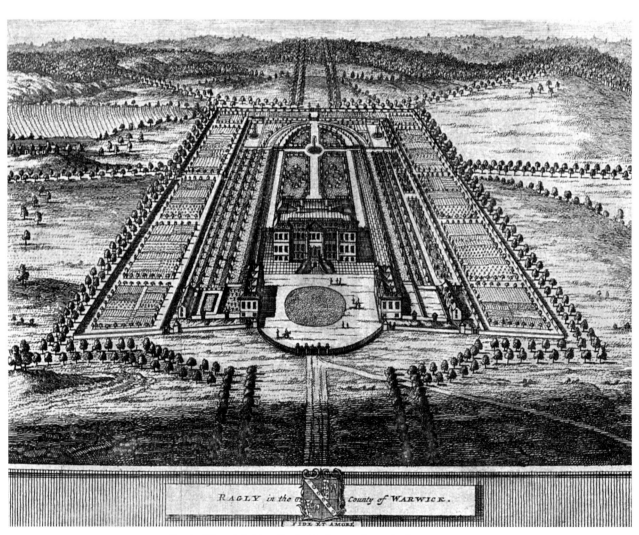

Ragly, Warwickshire. Perfect balance about the house

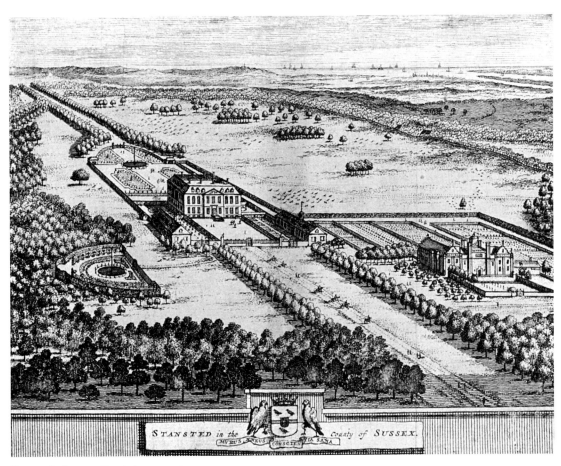

Stansted, Sussex. Partial asymmetry

Villa d'Este, Tivoli. From a print by Piranese

Garden of Carl Milles, near Stockholm. A dominant floor pattern holding together a variety of architecture

the view must have been a very secondary background. At Little Thakeham the pattern of the garden is actually unbalanced until it is seen that in reality the view gives the interest not seen on plan; its presence is here a necessity for comfort and repose. At times the garden becomes so overpowering as to dominate the house. This is a fine conception, a triumph of nature, and the house takes its place in a position arranged for it by the lay-out. The power of the garden at the Villa Lante at Bagnaia is so great that the house has been divided into two pavilions to allow it to flow in between. They are placed at the point of balance, but the climax of the scheme is in the four figures rising from the square water-garden. While the garden may be so overpowering, at times it dwindles away, as in a town garden, practically to disappear. Here it is so slight as hardly to affect the stability of the house. In its effect upon design, the relation in size between a house and its garden may vary to any extent, provided that the emphasis of either in the final scheme is no more than its importance will admit. The main lines of a composition laid out axially are usually a question of adjustment along the lines of balance. In a scheme where there is no apparent axis, the spaces of the garden are arranged in the same way as in a picture, linking themselves rhythmically round the point of balance. The gables that chase each other round a mediaeval house suggest a garden that follows their fancy. At Marshcourt, where the house is built on asymmetrical grouping, the parts of the garden reflect its balanced character arranging

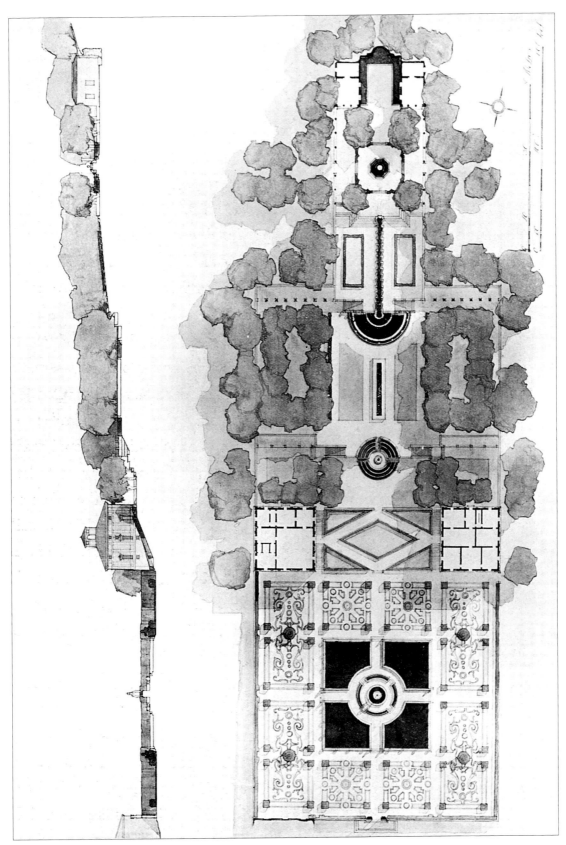

Villa Lante, Bagnaia. (By Vignola.) A delicately proportioned pattern, where there are no conflicting side interests to be subdued (compare with p.54). The division of the house into two pavilions emphasises the garden

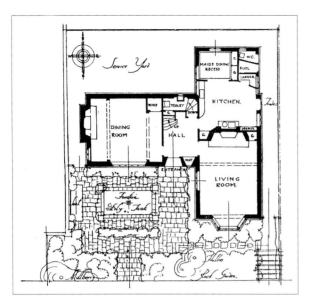

House at Wimbledon. (By P. D. Hepworth, F.R.I.B.A.) Close assocation in character between house and garden

Holmbury St. Mary. (By Oliver Hill, F.R.I.B.A.) Character of the house carried into the garden

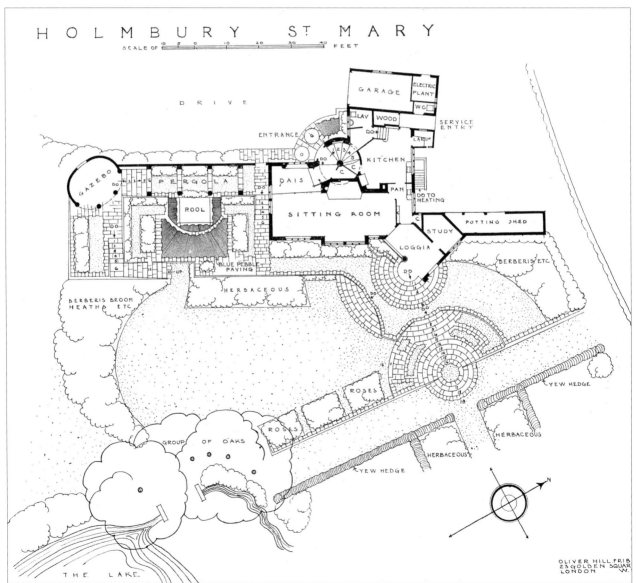

House at Holmbury St. Mary. (By Oliver Hill, F.R.I.B.A.) Grouping in perspective

themselves round the house, and held together by slender lines of circulation. A garden laid out symmetrically from an asymmetrical house may be incongruous unless it is flung sufficiently far away and there is a suggestion in between of a connection. However small the subject, these less sophisticated compositions suggest endless variety of arrangement, drawing upon the plan of the house itself for their inspiration. There is the simple little scheme at Wimbledon, or the more rhythmic one at Holmbury St. Mary; those that have more elements and perhaps use a loggia to connect house and garden; or the pattern in a confined town garden.

From the flat pattern of the garden, there is little consideration to encourage grouping and massing of its elements. A garden has as much solidity as building, and one that is purely pattern is like a house that is purely façade. It lacks substance, and becomes artificial. In a level country where the masses are planted on the ground, they have to be made and are disposed at will. Clipped trees and hedges take their places as solids, as in a smaller way do free-growing trees and bushes. Where the country is uneven and the garden is built in terraces, there is the chance of handling vast masses in a way inconceivable in any other branch of art. On Isola Bella the mass of the house balances the great rock-hewn terraces at the further

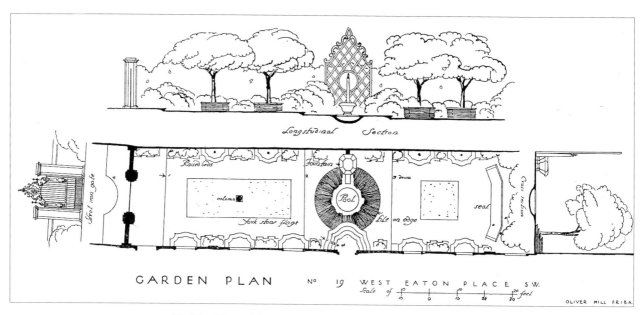

19, West Eaton Place, S.W. (By Oliver Hill, F.R.I.B.A.) Treatment of a confined site

extremity of the island. For the moment the terraces at the Villa d'Este at Tivoli piling up to the house strike the beholder dumb with wonder. Perhaps more than anyone else Frank Lloyd Wright in America has grasped the colossal latent power that lies behind the subject, using it in the smallest composition. If this grouping and massing bears out the flat pattern, and the pattern is itself interesting and unified, the feeling that results from walking about the garden will be indirectly the same. There is a sense of completeness in the transition of passing through the various spaces, whether between the masses or upon them. Each new space may in itself be interesting, or surprising, or exhilarating, but it is never out of place. It is, on the contrary, the note that has to be struck to complete the unity of the whole. Moreover, in perspective these designs fall naturally in good compositions. Definitely arranged viewpoints are liable to sacrifice everything to one end: and from the famous view in the circle of cypresses at the Villa d'Este to that of such a small group as the one at Holmbury St. Mary, fine effects have nearly always come first from a well-balanced plan. It is generally accepted that the grandest conceptions of the past were *considered* in perspective, but *designed* in plan or elevation. Gardens sometimes spread beyond their sphere, and attach themselves not only to external natural objects, but to buildings as well. Often in an English garden when the village clusters round the church, the tower or steeple has become part of the scheme. At Westbury the curious free-standing spire once finished the cross axis of the garden, and was then a foil to the long, low lines. The noblest example comes from the herbaceous walk at Salisbury, where a finer foreground to the Cathedral could scarcely be imagined. When a little garden like the one in Ampthill has to be absorbed by the town, it needs all the force of its corner piers to assert any independence within. The little communal garden at Hampstead Garden Suburb links across the road. These are intimate relationships, but often one finds a great garden embracing a very much wider area: the Villa Lante and the town of Bagnaia, the Farnese and the Farnesina palaces connected across the Tiber, Le Nôtre's scheme for the Champs Elysée, and in England, where such ideas have been less developed than abroad, perhaps Hampton

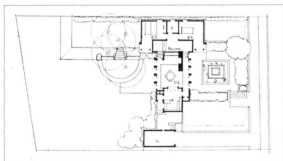

House in America. (By Frank Lloyd Wright.) A study in form

Court and Bushey Park.

The block form, with the parts waiting to be emphasised by detail, is the basis of a garden design. The decoration of this has to be consistent, for the quality of a small detail may make or mar a design. Close to, the eye first grasps detail, and if this earliest introduction to the garden is pleasing, it will proceed to the parts that really matter. The character of a place embraces house and garden, and the two work together so that it is difficult to say where the one leaves off and the other begins. Design seizes upon the necessary characteristics of both, shakes them together, and stamps itself equally upon every portion of the result; though it is true that often such an apparently small point as a vigorous floor pattern can draw together

29, Palace Street, S.W.1. (By L.H. Bucknell and R. Ellis)

many diverging parts. Perhaps the strongest thread that links the elements together is scale. Scale, related as it is to humanity, brings everything to a common standard of size, that presented by a man. It is not merely that the details give the proper sense of size to the parts, but all sorts of odd shapes and sizes are thus drawn together. Scale is that to which the eye is accustomed. The height of a balustrade, the size of a window or a door opening, a step, are all more or less fixed by utility. Details are fixed by the capability of material. Stone can be hewn in greater blocks than it is convenient to make a brick, but it cannot be carved to as fine a pitch as wood. A standard that is once accepted is used consistently throughout. Only where the parts are definitely separated, as in the secret garden of an entertaining garden, is it safe to juggle with different scales. The detail reflects the character of the pattern, from the light and graceful treillage that so delightfully expresses the plan of a French garden to the massive simplicity of the yews at Ven House. It is incongruous to have a refined shape on a rough ground, though a graceful form contrasts harmoniously enough with a refined strength of surface. Stateliness mates with delicacy,

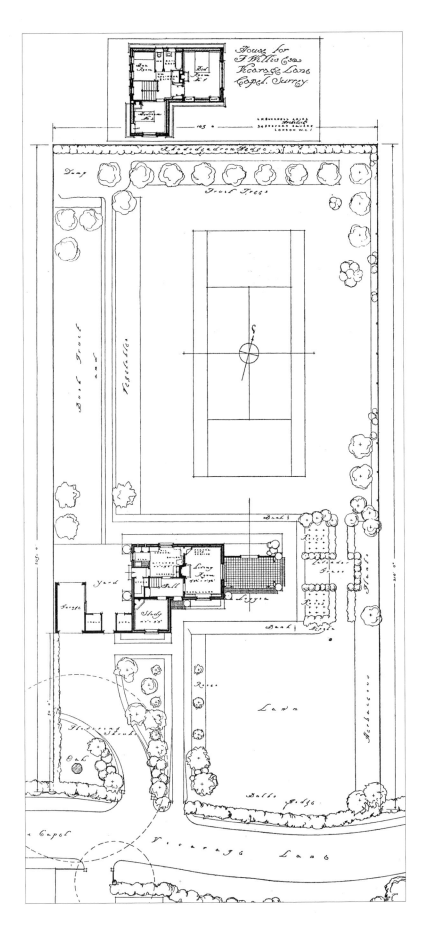

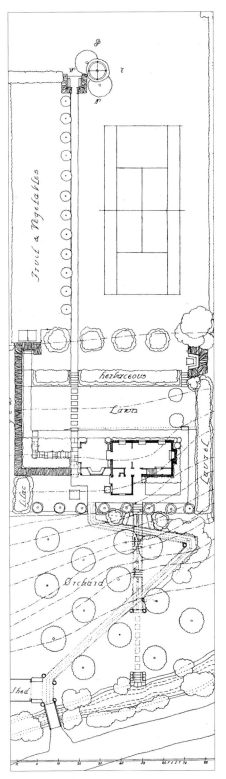

Cottage at Thornton-in-Cleveland, Yorkshire. A scheme suggested by contours and an exposed situation

House at Capel, Surrey. (By L.H. Bucknell, A.R.I.B.A.) Composition suggested by necessities

Salisbury: Garden in the Close. A composition of garden and cathedral, where unity in scale is gained by perspective

House at Ampthill. Relation of garden to village street

Hampstead Garden Suburb. Communal garden scheme connecting across the road

Ven House, Somerset. Topiary work expressing the character of English design

crude strength with wild fragility. The position of materials suggests their own treatment; a retaining wall may be formed of rugged jointed stonework, because this treatment suggests strength, though we know that a smooth surface would be equally strong. The retaining wall supports a pergola which by contrast is light and free, though not so free as to appear detached. Construction is often the clue to aesthetics, and we realise that the arch is so shaped to span a greater width than the lintel. The quality of the detail harmonises with the character of the garden; a balustrade is more refined than a brick wall and plain parapet. The materials used are also in keeping, and for this reason so refined a material as marble is out of place in an English garden, while it may be at home at Versailles. Bronzes and lead take on a beautiful texture if left to weather. Sculpture may seek to express not only the natural surroundings, but also architecture, and, apart from its texture, its design is something different from the mortal whose form it appears to take for the moment. It stands for an abstract idea, and may therefore assume a shape that expresses this idea rather than exact human form. The figure in the garden of the townhall at Stockholm is clearly a part of the building. When sculpture is actually carved on the building, it is still more closely related to the architecture. The first thing that matters in Epstein's panel on the monument to Hudson in Hyde Park is the architectural pattern of light and shade, which, foiled by its plain ground, attracts the eye immediately. The rhythm of shadows suggests the movement of wings, and design is unaffected by the sentiment of the subject. The simplification of form undoubtedly draws the subject to its

Above: Figure before the Stockholm Town Hall
Below: The Hudson Memorial, Hyde Park. (By Adams, Holden and Pearson: panel by
Jacob Epstein)
Relation of sculpture to architecture by attitude and treatment

Nîmes, the Public Garden. Convention in sculpture

Villa Bombicci, near Florence. Conventional relation of sculpture to architectural setting by attitude

architectural setting, but need not necessarily be emphasised to do this. A herm grows out of his base unconcernedly. In the lions that gaze out and frame the view from the Villa Bombicci, near Florence, attributed to Michaelangelo, the silhouette and form are related to their position mainly by their conventional attitude. Convention suggests topiary work, but only if it is as much related to the scheme as in the particular view of Compton Wynyates, or the more severe house at Moreton Valence, can it become essential. A detail preserves its freshness and spontaneity if it is designed for its place, for the finest detail becomes dead if it is in the wrong setting. A detail such as a moulding is again generally the outcome of purpose. The nosing to a garden step is for comfort, and its shape for strength. The line of shadow gives a refinement that a brick-on-edge step would lack. The overhang of a balustrade rail is given to throw off water, but its value lies in the refining shape that follows. The degree of refinement naturally varies. If the balustrade were coarse enough not to mind the weather, it follows that the position would also be coarse, and the lack of refinement justified. The principles of design are pattern. The light and shadow of a moulding is in reality an offspring of the pattern of the garden. A careful adjustment of detail will always blend together architecture of marked periods, though the varying types that go to make such a view as the approach vista at the Priory, Orpington, are necessarily assisted by time.

Horticulture has the same relation to the garden as any material. Flowers

Above: House at Moreton Valence, Gloucestershire
Below: Compton Wynyates
Relation of topiary to architecture

The Priory, Orpington. Harmony of time

are lovely things that enhance the garden, rather than make it. Like everything else, they take the places for which they have been designed. They are marshalled into ranks to give a mass of colour, and planted single where the intimacy allows for an appreciation of their perfect form. Specimens are things of special interest rather than beauty; and because the garden is primarily not a museum, they, too, conform to the general plan, rubbing alongside their neighbours on their aesthetic merits only. The herbaceous border is where all flowers meet, and its broken patchwork quilt effect covers a very much larger area in the scheme than would be possible if it were composed of one type. At Orpington there are two such borders rising one above the other to a high wall. Within their firm lines the flowers are forever tumbling over one another in delicious profusion. Flowers at all times are delicate and their immediate setting is important in connecting them up with their more robust surroundings. The border at Great Maytham is admirably related to the broad lawn and formal architecture of the house. When daffodils grow in clusters at the foot of trees, they are informal and closely akin to nature. Gather them up and place them in a formal bed and it is contrast of firm lines and colour that returns them their value. A Dutch garden, of the type in Kensington Gardens, is a delightful and considered setting for flowers; the simple rectangle of terraces rises in tiers from the water's edge and is backed by the calm dark surround of the pleached alley. Here varying flowers are planted in masses that form a pattern of colour when seen as a whole, but where each flower can also be visited by the paths that lead round. In contrast to this, the little enclosed formal garden at Marshcourt is over-architectural for flowers, but scores because it is interesting all the year round. Different flowers like different positions; the more robust prefer positions of importance, and the more delicate have to be treated with care. Such small, delicate-scented flowers as pinks are happy in beds raised from the walk, inviting by their scent. A fruit garden suggests its own interesting ways of arrangement. So are the minute items of the pattern drawn together to conform to their unit and at the same time to be seen at their best.

The garden is a place at peace. Not only is it at peace with the house and

The Priory, Orpington. Profusion of flowers in a firm setting

The Priory, Orpington. (By C. E Hughes.) Flowers in steadying lines of architecture

its surroundings, but it is at peace within itself. There is the harmony of an all-presiding genius. Parts are liable to stray and be lost; others may meet and disagree; others are too much in agreement to the exclusion of everyone else. Then comes this spirit of the garden, which has to do with the garden itself, welding them all into a powerful whole. Through all the

Great Maytham, Kent. Flowers connected in architectural surroundings

Kensington Gardens. An enclosed setting for flowers

works of art the world has produced, design runs evenly, appearing again and again in different forms, in literature, music, or the plastic arts. Its principles never alter. Expressing the chequered pattern of our lives, it is itself pattern, whether read, heard, or seen, and the greatest and most intricate work of art is in reality built upon this simple thing. Pattern springs

Marshcourt, Hampshire. (By Sir Edwin Lutyens.) An enclosed garden of a permanent character

Foots Cray Place. Fruit garden with design of espaliers

from rhythm, playing variations upon the beats of the pulse and weaving many elements into one. It assumes a definite character. That strange hypnotism over the senses comes when the whole is finely proportioned, and proportion is as elusive as it is wonderful. A work may be sound and substantial in principle; take away its proportion, and away goes the life. The design now adopts the form for which it is conceived, and it becomes an expression of reason.

PART 2

I

VILLA GAMBERAIA

The Italian Renaissance marks the entrance of the modern world. Perhaps for the first time the delicate shades of a variety of minds were understood. In those days individuals stood out in brighter high lights than now, and to Italy one must turn to feel most clearly the charm of personality in a garden. Outwardly Italian gardens are the expression of their own countrymen; in spirit they are almost universal.

In the Middle Ages a man was part of a community. He had no thoughts of himself, for life was but a preparation, and the enjoyment of the present lay in the anticipation of the future. The first to find the individual was Dante, for Dante, though still mediaeval in subject, tells of the passions that fill the soul. In art, a little later, Giotto breathed life into Madonnas that had been beautiful symbols of the unattainable. The spirit spread over Italy, and in a short time man came universally into his own. The times were well fitted to the furthering of individuality, for Italy was divided into small states, controlled either by republics or petty despots. Under them individualism was encouraged to flourish for good or bad. The printing-press enabled people to evade the preaching of the Church, which had for long forbidden free thought. In natural science, exploration, and discovery, individuals were probing everywhere. Social intercourse became an art, the whole mode of living taking on a higher status; the streets of Florence were paved when those of London and Paris were squalid and unhealthy. In every branch of life this vitality occurred, culminating in the consideration of the individual by himself.

The accomplishments of Michaelangelo or Leonardo da Vinci are well known, but probably the most versatile of all men was the Florentine, Leo Battista Alberti. As an athlete he was unrivalled in Florence. He practised architecture, composed music, studied law, physics and mathematics, and learnt every sort of craft. He was an author of exceptional range, his works including Latin prose and elegies, various moral and philosophical works, speeches and poems; and writings on art that are standard. "But the deepest spring of his nature has yet to be spoken – the sympathetic intensity with which he entered into the whole life around him."* While men were perfecting themselves, some were writing either their own biography or that of others. Vasari's Lives are intimately associated with the personalities they describe. Cellini, setting down his own strange spirit, tells frankly of a mighty personality curiously mixed with good and evil. Following the study of mankind, the position to which he was now raised is contained in a speech by Pico della Mirandola on the dignity of man. " I have set thee," says the Creator to Adam, " in the midst of the world, that thou mayest the more easily behold and see all that is therein. I created thee a being neither heavenly nor earthly, neither mortal nor immortal only, that thou mayest be free to shape and overcome thyself . . . To thee alone is given a growth and a development depending on thine own free will. Thou bearest in thee the

* Burckhardt, 'The Renaissance in Italy'

Villa Medici, Fiesole

germs of a universal life."

Together with the discovery of man, came the discovery of nature. The beauty of nature as an influence for good was unappreciated in mediaeval days. Literature is a reflection of thought, and in that of the Middle Ages there seems to be little description of natural scenery. The pageantry of Crusades is described, but not the country through which the Crusaders passed. People who communed with nature even ran the risk of being burnt. The Italians fully understood and felt the glory of a distant view, and it imprinted itself vividly upon their sensitive souls. While Dante saw nature dimly, Petrarch sang of it untrammelled; it is said that during his stay among the woods at Reggio, the sudden sight of an impressive landscape affected him so deeply he resumed a poem he had long set aside. Alberti himself felt the powers of nature. ". . . at the sight of noble trees and waving cornfields, he shed tears . . . and more than once when he was ill, the sight of a beautiful landscape cured him."* It was love of nature and distant views that called the Florentines from town, prepared even to face the uncertain safety of the country in order to enjoy it to the utmost.

It followed that this highly developed and sensitive people soon turned their attention to the strengthening and refreshing of the mind. Of all the arts at their disposal gardens made the strongest appeal. In the days of Lorenzo de Medici at Florence, one reads of how the greatest minds loved to commune together in gardens. The Villa Medici at Fiesole still stands much as the first Cosimo built it, and on the broad terrace or in the loggia the Platonic Academy would meet to conduct their profound arguments in sight of the distant towers of Florence. These were the early attempts of expression in the garden, rising from the need of surroundings to give that enjoyment of the present so richly described by Boccaccio. All the intricate machinery of garden design was set to work, and through the fourteenth, fifteenth and sixteenth centuries design slowly advanced in the wake of knowledge. The sixteenth century is the golden age of Italian Renaissance art, but it was not until the following century that technique was able, or had the opportunity, to express the many sides of the mind in one garden. The long low lines of the Villa Medici carved out of the hill describe in their simple way the dignity of learning. The subtleties of a single personality are here lost in a wider range of expression. While expression in any work of art is highly complex, in gardens especially the personal side may be swamped by stronger outside influences. In the early part of the Renaissance, the

* Burckhardt, 'The Renaissance in Italy'

Villa Madama, Rome

whole outlook on life was coloured by the study of antiquity. Greek and Roman manuscripts were eagerly sought. The philosophy of the ancients became that of the day. All over Italy men turned to the ruins of ancient Rome to provide them with inspiration to build in the spirit of the new. Though at no time was native talent entirely overwhelmed by the influence of the humanists, up to the fifteenth century the finer shades of expression were lost. In the sixteenth century the humanists fell, and genius found its natural expression.

The Italians of the Renaissance were a passionate people. A whole city could be stirred by the elocution of one man, and then turn and send him to the stake. The strength that had made Rome mistress of the world was disseminated in internal strife. Individuals could not unite. The Romans were as fond of gardens as the Renaissance Italians, and without the sense of imperialism behind, such hills as the Palatine would not have been subdued so ruthlessly as they were. Rome produced great individuals, but never so great as to rival the empire. In the letters of Pliny are admirable descriptions of gardens and contemporary garden life. Pliny was an individualist, but his gardens were not his own so much as Roman, and because of this they surely overrode the subtler feelings of both himself and country. Having no great national force to express, and with ancient Rome by this time a shadow of the past, the later Tuscan gardens were able to mingle and present the very finest shades of individual and nature. Here lies the secret of their delicacy and charm.

The evolution of the Villa Gamberaia can be traced from the quattrocento Florentine gardens of Michelozzo that include the Villa Medici at Fiesole. From there, interest almost at once turns to Rome, soon eclipsing all other states in its rapid rise to power. In 1516, Cardinal Giuliano de Medici began the Villa Madama, which stands at the parting of the ways between the homeliness of Florence and the pomp of Rome. The papacy was now a mighty temporal as well as spiritual power. Mindful of the past to which they were heirs, the Princes of the Church began to build themselves homes on the lines of those of the Roman Empire. The Villa Madama was intended as a great house of entertaining just outside Rome, and though never completed, in its main lines is a pure reincarnation of antiquity. Few ancient Roman villas surpassed it in splendour of size or efficiency of planning. But the germ of individuality was abroad even under the cloak of a Cardinal, and in 1550, the most dramatic garden in Europe was undertaken at Tivoli for Cardinal Hippolito d'Este. The Villa d'Este is in no way equal in

Villa Torlonia, Frascati

technique or refinement to the Villa Madama. The power it expresses is that
of a Cardinal of the Church, but a touch of personality lightens it up and
gives it a forceful charm of its own. Though the terraces are simple to an
extreme, a host of means are employed to make the splendour of the whole
overwhelm the senses. After the completion of the Villa d'Este, design in
Rome developed rapidly. There was no such thing as a garden architect
distinct from an architect of building. The universality of the time realised
that the two arts were one, and it is therefore not strange to find that
Vignola, known to the world as architect of the Church of the Jesuits in
Rome, was also the genius of the greatest gardens of the latter half of the
century. Vignola's opportunity lay in expressing the grandeur rather than
the intimacy of the Roman Cardinals. The drama of the Villa d'Este is
accordingly an inspiration, though a superior mastery of technique
produced gardens of equal imagination and a greater refinement. The Villa
Lante at Bagnaia is carried out in every detail with perfect unity and
delicacy, and is possibly the finest of the gardens designed first for
entertaining. It was from the great gardens of Rome that France later drew
inspiration for developing the entertaining garden to its ultimate stage.

In Florence, which had been quietly progressing, the personal side of the
garden continued to develop in the wake of the individual. Villas round
Florence in the sixteenth century are supposed to have numbered
thousands. Apart from the Boboli gardens, scarcely one of them could have
been so striking or grand as the smallest of the handful at Frascati, outside
Rome. Each, however, contained an element of humanity that was its own.
In contrast to that of the Cardinals, the power of the Florentines lay to a
certain extent in the soil. The country villa often served as much for a farm
as for a pleasure-house, and thereby established a closer bond between man
and nature. To the north of Fiesole there is a villa, half farm, half pleasure-
house, where the garden wanders away up the hillside among freely planted
olive-trees. Stone steps, a seat, or a piece of rough terracing here and there
invite one onwards. It is the garden of an olive grove. The Florentine was
feeling his way to a place no less restfully composed but more gently har-
nessed than that of his Roman contemporary. The end of the sixteenth
century probably saw the larger proportion of gardens round Florence
asymmetrical in their planning, some of them haphazard in their stringing
together of formal parts, but others very wisely, if simply, composed in
relation to their surroundings. From all these sources, and to a certain
extent from the magnificent contemporary Roman planning, sufficient

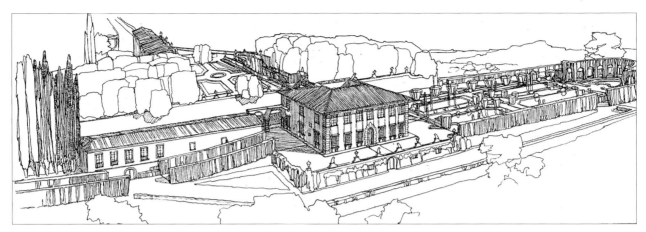

Villa Gamberaia

technique was acquired by the beginning of the seventeenth century to evolve the Villa Gamberaia.

Little is known of its history. A house was in existence in 1398, and early in the sixteenth century the famous Florentine and Sienese architects, the Rossellini, lived here with their father. The place as it stands today probably dates from about 1610.

The village of Settignano is some five miles east of Florence, on the lower slopes of the same range of hills that is crowned by Fiesole. Gamberaia lies on about the same level, and half a mile beyond. The lane passes the entrance, under a bridge that supports the long alley, and so on up the hill to one of those wayside altars where the valley of the Arno lies outstretched. On all sides nature teems with life. Here and there a villa or a farmhouse, marked by cypress, stands out white and homely on slopes of softly changing greys and greens. In the distance the blue hills gather round the city. For the moment the villa is out of sight, but lower down the lane it can be seen from above, spreading along the natural levels and bathed in sun.

The peculiarity of the site lay in the roads that enclose it on three sides. The shape filled is an elongated irregular area of little more than two acres. Privacy from the roads, with complete command of the view, is worked into a garden that has every variety in itself. It is due to the skilful planning that there hangs over the whole a sense of everlasting peace. The very simplicity of the materials that the Italian had at his disposal, evergreens, stone, and water, enabled him to be richer in the form of his pattern. The plan of Gamberaia is a masterpiece of composition. A long strip of grass, starting from the cypresses and leading out into the view, is stretched from one extremity to the other. The house is placed adjoining, and extends its façade in arches along it as if in sympathy with the great length. Round the house, binding the two still more firmly together, is a band of grass as broad as the alley. On the axis of the house, and lightly connected with it by a stone path, is a grotto garden. The composition of house, alley, and grotto is thus stabilised. It only remained to fill in the spaces of the pattern in such a way as not to disturb the balance. Of these, the water parterre is the most interesting feature, and this was balanced by a simple lemon garden, the block of outhouses, and the cypress garden that terminates the long alley. The boscos equalise themselves. The scheme is in perfect balance about a point that coincides with the fine east entrance door. As pattern design, the length of the alley contrasts with the square house and its interestingly

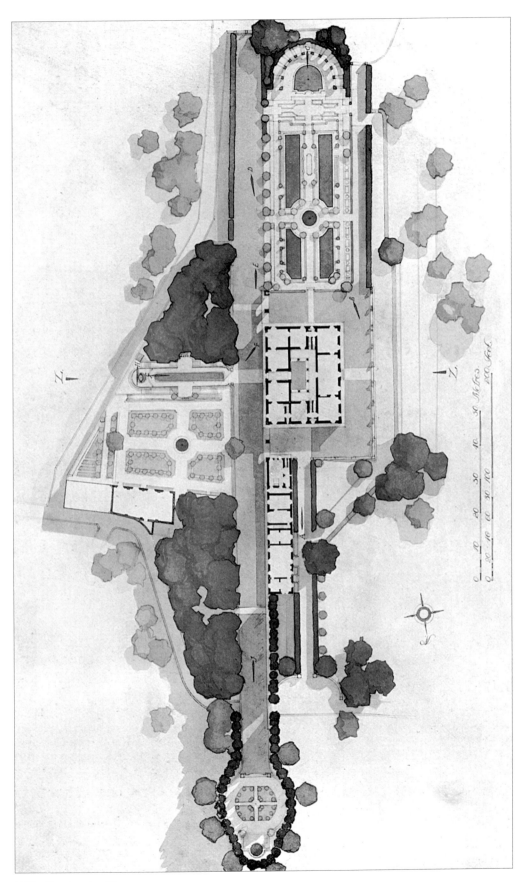

Villa Gamberaia. Plan

Villa Gamberaia. Elevation to west

Villa Gamberaia. Section Z-Z on plan

shaped grotto, which again contrast with themselves. The gardens inside the spaces are all foiled by the same simple alley and grass band. The plan is so contrived that no fewer than six or seven different gardens are within speaking distance of the house.

The approach to this beautiful place may have led down to an entrance in the wall below the main terrace, and people were able to come and go without in any way interfering with the garden immediately round the house. Before the west façade the broad simple terrace alone separates the building from the view. Stone dogs sitting on the low parapet break up a line that might be too abrupt, and mingle with the middle distance. Passing along this terrace, one enters the water garden, extending away from the south façade and enclosed from the view by dark walls of hedge. Differing slightly from the lines of the original design, everything in this garden is gay and fanciful. Low box hedges and shapes are dotted in neat array, and pools reflect the sky or buildings. Over all there is the note of singing frogs, blending together in a paean of praise. From this garden one passes through clipped yews into the long alley. Pico della Mirandola's words on the dignity of man are recalled in this stately walk. To the right it sweeps out across the balustrade into the distance; to the left it passes between the east wall of the house and the retaining walls of the lemon garden, and disappears into the shadows of the cypress grove. Now one approaches the entrance to the grotto garden, and pride has its fall; the place is frankly grinning. Up the steps one scrambles on to the lemon garden, where the air blows briskly. Beyond this lies the mystery of the ilex bosco, of twisted trunks

Villa Gamberaia. The Approach: Viewpoint A on plan

Villa Gamberaia. The Terrace: Viewpoint B on plan

Villa Gamberaia. The Water Garden: Viewpoint C on plan

Villa Gamberaia. The Long Alley: Viewpoint D on plan

Villa Gamberaia. The Long Alley: Viewpoint E on plan

Villa Gamberaia. Approach to Grotto Garden: Viewpoint F on plan

Villa Gamberaia. The Grotto Garden: Viewpoint G on plan

Villa Gamberaia. The Lemon Garden: Viewpoint H on plan

and tangled branches that exclude the sky. Through this one passes out again to the spaciousness of the alley, and so into the cypress grove, where the slender ethereal forms cluster round and whisper of eternity.

Throughout the garden the scale varies with the mood of the moment. The house itself is a perfect example of Florentine art in its proportions and restraint. In its solidity it stands for ever amidst a slowly changing garden. The scale of the house is to our modern ideas more than human, but in those days must have attuned to their highly developed minds. The scale of the terrace before the house is as broad as the view, in the water garden it is slightly lowered, is regained in the bowling alley, becomes reduced to the ridiculous in the grotto garden, and finishes intensely intimate to great and small alike in the bosco. Colour everywhere is a symphony of greens from deep cypress through varieties of box, yew, ilex, and privet, to the light emerald of lemon-trees and grass. The house is a broken ivory, and is spread through the green around in paving, balustrades, walls, and statuary. Like so many gardens of Florence, the soft cool colour takes the place of shade as a protection against the sun. Practically the only considered shade, apart from the cypress garden, are the boscos, placed with immediate access from the house. Shape and form are consistent; the square, blunt house is

Villa Gamberaia. The Cypress Grove: Viewpoint J on plan

supported by firm lines of architecture and clipped evergreens. Though the boscos practically adjoin the house, and are themselves the embodiment of nature running free, they are enclosed almost to their full height by walls. Branches meet overhead, and the simple shape of the ilex above provides in effect a formal roof spanning from wall to wall. Few other trees would be so suitable to their position. The tall slender cypresses are ever present, as splendid a foil in fact to the long horizontal lines that bind the garden to the ground as they are in association and spirit. Above all, for over three hundred years nature has been slowly working her will, breaking the hard lines of architecture, enriching the garden with interest, and binding all together inextricably.

To step into this garden is to mingle with a personality intensely alive and human, one that shunned ostentation and was not afraid to admit weakness. This mind felt all the passions of the soul that filled the noblest Italians, answering as readily to the peace of nature.

II

LE NÔTRE AT VERSAILLES

To pass into France from Italy in the seventeenth century was to cross a barrier more dividing than the Alps. Louis XIV reigned in state. If Louis smiled, France smiled with him; if Louis frowned, France frowned and trembled. When he walked abroad, picking his way in satin shoes, all France hung upon his steps and lightly cleared the path. It was a time when elegance, wit, and charm were welcome everywhere, and to them the monarch was ever at home in the gardens of Versailles.

The gesture of contempt that Louis made to the world, he made to the country round his palace. The greater the difficulties, the more wealth was poured forth to overcome them. For years whole armies of men and horses toiled and sweated in turning earth and carting stone. The lake extending beyond the Orangery was dug out of a fever-stricken marsh, causing appalling loss of life to the Swiss Guards who made it. Behind the gigantic work of the gardens lay that of bringing water to the fountains. The supply

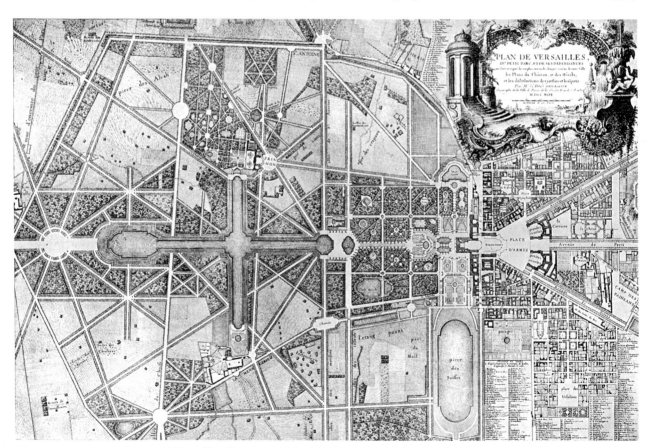

Versailles. From a plan by the Abbé Delagrive, dated 1746

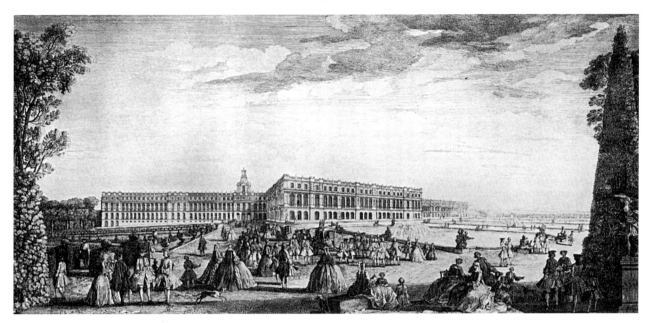

Versailles

from local sources soon failed, and a scheme was devised for raising the water of the Seine under its own power up to an aqueduct at Marly, seven miles away. Louis was delighted, and in 1685 water was pouring into Versailles. Even this was insufficient. At once he determined on the more ambitious task of tapping the Eure below Chartres. Thirty thousand soldiers were employed, and in two years a canal reached Maintenon. The work of spanning the valley was commenced but never finished, for war then broke out. Forty-eight scarcely completed arches, each thirty metres high, are today as an impressive a monument to the monarch as Versailles itself. These enormous efforts were put into a garden that was to be a perfect setting for the Sun King and his Court. The dark side, the loss of life and the enormous expense that crippled the whole country, gave way to pleasure. Any hot summer's day was sufficient to draw people from palace and town. All who were "reasonably dressed" were admitted to the park, and countrymen's carts jostled those of noblemen.

On the plage before the palace the crowds moved slowly along terraces and walks, the full skirts of women contrasting with the elegant forms of men. If you followed the stateliest group of people, you would see Louis the most perfectly dressed and stately of them all. When they disappeared down the alleys into the bosquets, and the woods threw back their cries, it was Louis who inspired the gaiety. These were the days before youth was lost, and Madame de Maintenon came to sober the Court. When the King and his party voyaged on the grand canal, they could choose a barge or any of the thirty gondolas. Perhaps they would go to the Menagerie to see the elephant and camels, or perhaps to the opposite arm to visualise a Trianon. When they disembarked, sedan chairs and even coaches were at hand to carry home those who wearied of the endless paths and avenues. In the evening, after a rest, a collation might be taken in one of the bosquet gardens. Weird and wonderful designs in dishes arrived, brought by light-footed servants who slipped through the trees and away, and were scarcely seen at all. In the woods around soft music played. Afterwards, perhaps, our party moved on to the circular colonnade, there like wraiths in the

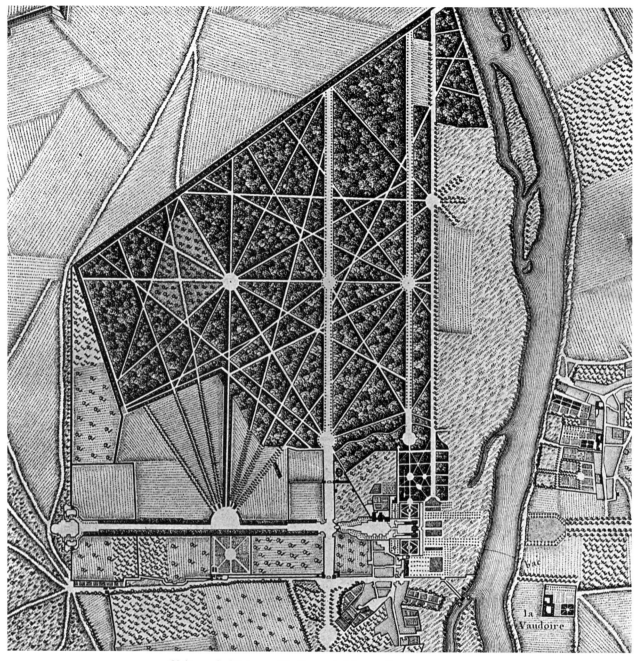

Château de Maisons. (By François Mansart)

moonlight to dance round and round to the murmur of fountains, until the moon paled and the stars began to fade. Sometimes there was a fête, and the whole of the gardens stirred themselves. Imagine the great fête of 1664. It lasted three days, and consisted of a pageant entitled "The Pleasures of the Enchanted Isle." First of all, gaily dressed knights tilted up and down the Tapis Vert, at that time an alley of beaten earth. Then a pageant was formed and wound in and out of the walks. The Chariot of Time led off, and was followed by the Centuries and Seasons, with dancing fauns, bacchantes, shepherds and shepherdesses, and Pan bringing up the rear. On the second day the principal feature was Molière's play "Princesse d'Elide." In the evening of the third day, all flocked to the basin of Apollo. Here was an

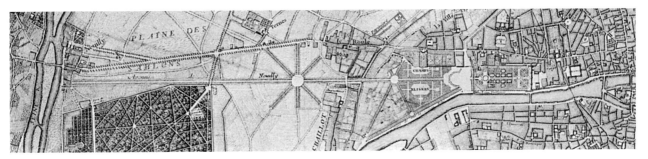

The Tuileries and Champs Elysées in 1740

island, and on the island stood an enchanted castle, which belonged to no less a person than the redoubtable sorceress who held Ruggiero in captivity. Excitement waxed intense. Three ladies advanced from the island reciting verses, two of them poised on the backs of whales, and one on a sea monster. A burst of fireworks then engulfed the island, consumed them all, and so finished the ballet. People dispersed, and the fête was over.

These were the gardens in the height of their glory. History shows that not even the Grand Trianon, built in 1670 and a few years later pulled down and rebuilt, could satisfy the King's passion for novelty. He settled on Marly, a beautiful whim that was to cost nearly as much as the gardens of Versailles.

Garden design in France begins along the banks of the Loire. In the early Renaissance Paris was turbulent, and the remoteness of the Touraine combined with the beautiful country to call there Francis I and his Court. The King loved building. His campaign in Italy may not have been a success politically, but it gave him a vital insight into the Renaissance. For a long time, however, tradition in France held out against the Italian architects and craftsmen who returned with him, and only in detail was the Italian influence noticeable. The châteaux of the day were mediaeval castles with elegant trimmings. If the châteaux had little understanding of the contemporary Italian villa, the garden had still less. Gardens were laid out, but happening to go beyond an enclosure, they only did so to spread round the walls in simple squares with little relation to the buildings themselves. These romantic places created the two traditions of water and avenues that were to influence the whole future of French gardens. It was reflections and association that a little later induced Philibert de l'Orme to stretch the new wing of Chenonceaux across the Cher. The tradition of avenues rose from hunting on a scale that the Italians never achieved. Great forests were preserved, and avenues and vistas cut through from end to end in a network of ways. At first the ways were utilitarian, but from them sprang the co-ordination in planning that is behind not only the gardens, but the towns and cities of France. Towards the end of the sixteenth century Paris offered more attractions, and the Court slowly moved from the Loire. Italian influence now became marked. The planning of house, garden, and forest began to be considered as one unit. In 1642, François Mansart designed the Château de Maisons near Paris, where the fine avenue approach to the house connects to a scheme of avenues in the forest.

With the accession of Louis XIV, that proud monarch concentrated on building, and in Le Nôtre found a lieutenant worthy of carrying unity to its supreme stage. André Le Nôtre was born in Paris in 1615. He died in 1700, not having known a day's illness. From the first he had every opportunity. His father was head gardener in the Tuileries, and sent André into the studio of Simon Vouet. Here he not only learnt something of composition,

Vaux-le-Vicomte

but probably began a friendship with Charles Le Brun, a fellow-student, which proved invaluable in after life. One of his earliest works was the addition to the Tuileries. By this he extended the Palace from within the city to beyond the Bois de Boulogne, at that time far outside the walls. This scheme is the Champs Elysées and the Place de l'Etoile of today. Then came Vaux-le-Vicomte for Fouquet, the first of the great spectacular gardens. The wealth of parterre, statues, and fountains that lies before the château windows is magnificently staged between varying widths and on levels that conceal surprises. Nothing of its kind had ever before been attempted in France. On August 17, 1661, Fouquet gave his great fête; a few days later he was thrown into prison. His morals were doubtful, but not his artistic perception. Vaux fired the King's ambition sufficiently not only to contemplate garden design on a vast scale, but eventually to move to Versailles the three creators of Vaux, Le Vau the architect, Le Brun the decorator, and Le Nôtre, the garden designer.

In 1663, Le Nôtre was commissioned to add gardens to Chantilly, the home of the great Condé. The existing château, mostly destroyed, but since rebuilt, stood surrounded by a broad moat. Around this again lay the forest of Chantilly, crossed and recrossed by its avenues. Le Nôtre grasped his material, saw that the scale of the château was unequal to his ideas, and made the centre of his conception the statue of the Condé. The design is brilliant. The soldier stands out as nobly among his possessions as he did in the forefront of battle. The great cross axis drives into the heart of the forest on the one side, and on the other carries through the arm of the canal. The

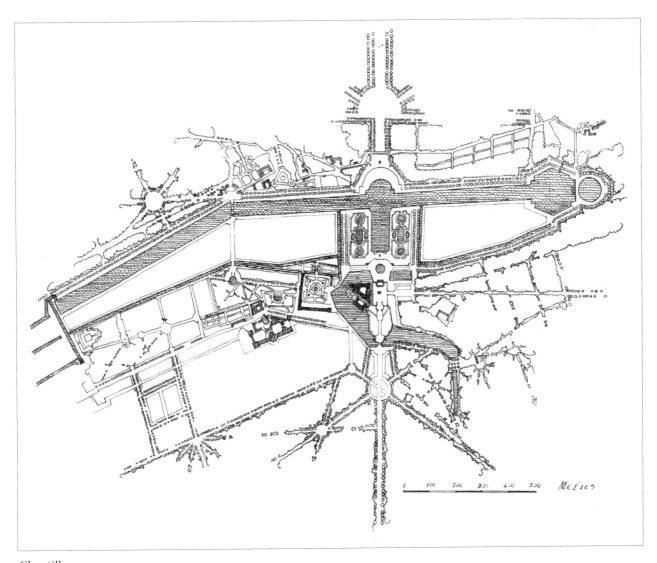

Chantilly

vast extent of the canal is associated with the house by water parterre and
moat. The fêtes that were held here on the canals and in the woods,
splendid as they were, were but a prelude to those held at Versailles. It is
said that while Vaux brought fame to Le Nôtre, it was Chantilly that decided
the King to entrust him immediately with his own gardens. The age of
Versailles did not allow many such places. The King ruled supreme from his
bed, and on his favour often depended the very substance of the nobles.
Under the artificiality, wigs and paint and powder, there lay an element of
power that made France the first country in Europe. Louis had a genius for
choosing the man for the position. Newly risen ministers reflected in a
milder way the ideas of their master, and while the old nobility were wasting
themselves at Versailles, they almost alone, outside royalty, undertook any
serious building. For them, as well as for the King's family, Le Nôtre
designed gardens in the environs of Paris on a scale that is stupendous.

Besides Vaux and Chantilly, Sceaux with its beautiful cascade and canal
was built for Colbert. A view terrace a mile and a half in length was added
to the existing garden at St. Germain. At Meudon, for the Grand Dauphin,
a still more titanic scheme was extended across the country. At St. Cloud,

Chantilly. From the south

another royal palace, the park was turned into a garden of avenues with cascades and pools. The activities of Le Nôtre were immense and spread beyond France into England and Italy, carrying everywhere some spirit of the pomp of Versailles. The genius of the man suited the age. He himself was not fond of Court life. When the King, with whom he was a favourite, wished to present him with a coat of arms, he protested that he already had one: "Three snails and a cabbage ball in chief, and how can I leave out my spade?" He supplied the background which artists of the time touched up

Chantilly. From the north

Cascade at Sceaux

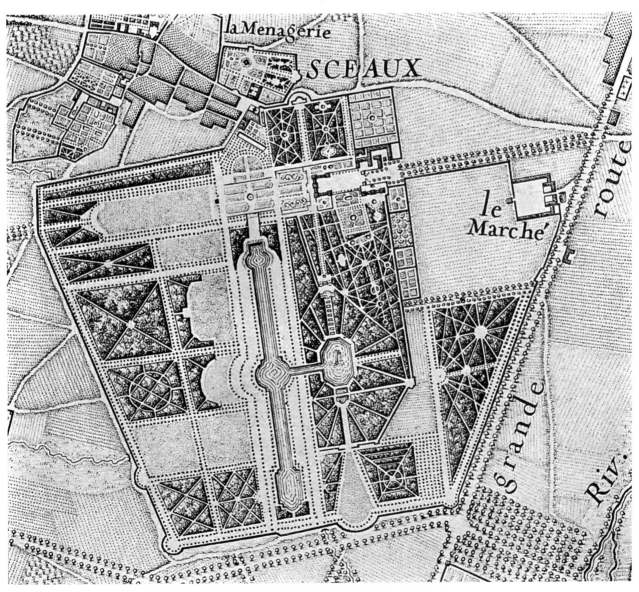

Sceaux

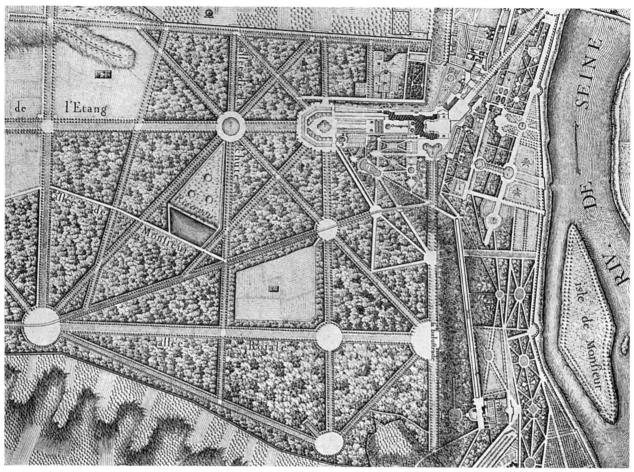

St. Cloud

so delicately. By himself he was as bold as was the King beneath his courtliness. His ideas embraced whole areas of country and bent them to his will. When it came to adding on to existing works, he did not attune his scale to theirs. He either put them in their place, as at Chantilly; or frankly ignored them, as at Meudon or Fontainebleau. The two spectacular features that he played with and perfected in nearly every garden were the old traditions of avenues and water.

When Louis XIV first came to Versailles, it consisted of a hunting-box built for Louis XVIII. From the first the hunting and situation attracted him. Le Vau was commissioned to enlarge the existing château, and a suggestion of the gardens as they stand today began to appear in the forest around. Visits increased in number and duration until at last the place became almost his permanent home. With the increase of power and the consequent extension of the Court, his ambitions in regard to it expanded. In 1679, while Le Nôtre was carrying on steadily with the gardens, Hardouin Mansart was commissioned completely to transform Le Vau's little château, and to make it worthy of the greatest monarch in Christendom.

The gardens mark one of the highest epochs in pattern design. Except in the main levels, which could not be avoided, in the view towards the Satory Woods, and in the choice of trees, the lay-out has no relation to the country. The whole scheme might be a piece of embroidery, its end pinned to the ground by the radiating avenues of the *étoile*. Trees are marshalled in

The Canal at Fountainebleau

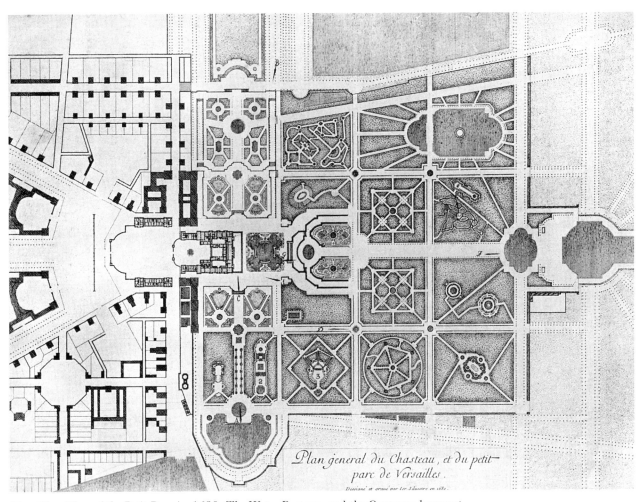

Plan general du Chasteau, et du petit parc de Versailles.

Dessine et gravé par Ier Silvestre en 1680.

Versailles. Plan of the Petit Parc in 1680. The Water Parterre and the Orangery have not yet been altered, and the Circular Colonnade, Viewpoint E, has not been constructed

Versailles. The Tapis Vert and the Grand Canal: Viewpoint G on plan

Versailles. The Grand Canal in the Time of Louis XIV

Versailles. Approach of the Hundred Steps: Viewpoint B on plan

thousands, and count not as individuals but as masses. In mere size the gardens surpass anything of their kind in Europe. Scale, however, is independent of size, and the scale of French art of the period is essentially intimate and charming. This is emphasised at Versailles, where the scale of the Palace was set by Le Vau's refronting of the earlier building. Mansart's Galeries des Glaces and the two wings increase the frontage but not the scale. Spreading outwards from this façade, the scale of the parts of the gardens gradually increases until it reaches the huge element of the Grand Canal. By simplifying the distance the increasing scale adds to the drama of the central vista, round which the garden builds. Similarly the hundred steps and the Orangery widen out, more abruptly, to the view across the Swiss Lake. The gravelled walks, especially near the Palace, are sufficiently wide for coaches to pass comfortably, yet the vases and sculpture of these parts are scarcely more than life-size. Across the expanse of gravel they were intended to be connected one to another by people; without people, and especially those in the costumes of the period, the design is incomplete. Where an Italian garden with its greater scale and smaller size as a rule needs a single person, a French garden needs the vivacity of crowds.

The water parterre of the Palace with its twin pools and exquisite sculpture plants the glittering façade on the ground, while the raised position almost on a level with surrounding trees, gives a spaciousness far beyond its size. The water parterre troubled Le Nôtre and an earlier and more elaborate scheme was altered in favour of the present. Nothing could

Versailles. The Grand Canal: Viewpoint F on plan

Versailles. The Satory Woods: Viewpoint C on plan

Versailles. In the Bosquets: Viewpoint D on plan

be finer than this introduction to the vista that emerges over its brim. Generations continue to be inspired by the view. Every moment it changes. Shadows travel up its length, emphasising plane after plane of trees. The Grand Canal lays a great length of sky upon the ground. On beyond, the ground runs up in grass, and the distant country is narrowed and framed by twin rows of poplars that appear as one. The handling of widths, materials, and levels is superb. Immediately below one lies the fountain of Latona, round which spread the lines of circulation. Today the effect is altered by the yew trees that have outgrown their size, the meagre parterre,

Versailles. The Circular Colonnade: Viewpoint E on plan

Versailles. The Dragon Fountain and Allée d'Eau: Viewpoint A on plan

and the untidiness of the surrounding trees. Once Louis XIV mapped out a route to show the gardens to guests, and he would stand and admire the Palace from the south-west corner of the parterre, with people streaming down the stairs and ramps. On the right of the Palace the sloping parterre is enclosed except for the avenue leading to the fountain and basin of Neptune. This avenue is one of the most delightful features of the park. On the left, the axis crosses another parterre, wide open to the Satory Woods across the Swiss Lake. The elaborate parterre competes with the view, does not in any way reflect it, and both become an integral part of the garden only when one is seen without the other. Walks, as though carved out of the trees, were once lined with "charmilles," hedges of hornbeam grown on treillage. These averaged about twenty-five feet high, and in the early days entirely dominated the growing trees they enclosed. People rarely penetrated into the spaces between. The statues and hermæ that follow the walks stood out against the walls of green, whose firm line connected one to another. The white flecks of stone give the size to the parts and extend the Palace into the Bosquets.

It seems that Le Brun and Le Nôtre together decided upon the position and type of sculpture, and the sculptor was then given free rein to his fancies. At the intersection of the cross walks in the Bosquets, the sculpture in the circular basins is kept low not to interfere with the vistas, and is closely related to the immediate foliage. The sculpture here is scarcely less sophisticated than that by the Palace; it gives an idea of the formality of planting that it does not appear out of place. Most of the gardens in the Bosquets have disappeared, but there is one, the circular colonnade, that is in almost perfect condition. By itself, it is, perhaps, the most beautiful piece of architecture at Versailles. The materials are of the finest, and the slender marble columns echo the trees among which they stand. But the life of the gardens is water. Today the fountains are still except for an hour or two on occasional Sundays, though the pools continue to mirror either their surroundings or the sky. It is the sky in the water that increases the sense of space on the terrace before the Palace. Flanking either side of the way down

Versailles. The Water Theatre: Viewpoint 3 on plan

to the parterre of Latona are two small partially enclosed tanks, the water level only two or three feet below eye level. These are the contrast. In the Bosquets the pools double the trees, increasing the height of avenues. So many fountains have gone that prints alone can recall them, or tell of the song of water that percolated everywhere. Giant spouts flung water into the air in masses. Tiny jets wove graceful patterns with their neighbours. The Dragon spouted in constant rage. Children of the woods for ever played in showers of rain. Though the water is silent, the bronzes and marbles are scarcely older than when Louis saw them. The trees are in their fourth generation, as fresh and young as ever. Over them hangs the spirit of perpetual youth, that deceived the Court in the passage of time. The Grand Canal seems alone to hold the history of the years: when the sunshine is playing upon the waters, or when the clouds roll up dark and threatening. Twilight finds it calm and thoughtful, brooding on the past.

Versailles. Les Trois Fontaines: Viewpoint 2 on plan

III

THE ENGLISH TRADITION

HISTORY

Italy found a great art expression during the Renaissance, France culminated under Louis XIV. In the history of England there seems to be no one period that can be definitely singled out and described as the summit of her artistic achievements. The history has been one chequered by foreign influences. The straight roads across Britain tell of the ruthless power of the first Romans, and such remains of villas suggest that these were in spirit but outposts of the Empire. The Normans found a nation more developed and better able to survive a new influence. Through the Middle Ages, though the Mother Church of Westminster Abbey was rebuilt under French influence, the country was steadily creating a tradition of art which culminated in domestic work in the sixteenth century. Probably it is from the time of Henry VIII to Elizabeth, when the first uncertain indications of the Renaissance from Italy were being felt, that England was most independent. By the time of Charles I the Italian influence was reaching its most marked period. Under Charles II and the Restoration the close intercourse between France and England meant the introduction into this country of the pronounced ideas of Le Nôtre, and this continued, with a brief interlude under William and Mary, during and after the French wars in the reign of Queen Anne.

COUNTRY & CLIMATE

If the history has been varied, to unroll the map of England is to see an equally varied landscape. Every county has its own characteristic. There are the flats of Norfolk and Suffolk contrasting with the Peak District of Derbyshire, the spirited outline of the Cleveland hills in Yorkshire with the more sober lines of the South Downs, the richly wooded agricultural land of Devonshire with the wildness of the adjoining moors. All over the country the scenery changes every few miles, and because for the most part buildings have been made from the most accessible materials, there is a constant change in their combination. Where the district has no stone (and the types of stone are innumerable) brickwork has been brought to a high pitch of design, as in the old mansions of Essex. The half-timbered houses of Cheshire and elsewhere suggest well-wooded areas. In the fen districts materials were limited to what could be brought on horseback, for there were no good roads. Before the beginning of the eighteenth century every part of the country had its own crafts, often handed down from family to family, and architecture, filtering through slowly from the nearest centre of fashion, was considerably affected by local traditions; at the time of Henry VII, when the history of the English garden begins to take shape, craftsmanship in this country was in many ways unequalled in Europe. In considering all this variety of landscape and materials in England, there is one element that appears not only to weld everything together, but to be so strong an influence in itself that it may have controlled the whole course of English garden design. The hedges and fields that chequer the country before ever a garden is made cast over the land a certain degree of formality. In time the garden grew to fill the spaces, and at last it broke the lines and swept them away from its path, as though a hindrance rather than an inspiration.

Climate has been another influence. It is a sombre country, more winter than summer, and because of this the relation of house to garden has altered considerably from time to time. At first there are massive walls and tiny windows to keep out the cold, directly opposed to a similar proportion in Italy, so arranged to keep out the heat. As time goes on the windows grow wider, and there are separate fireplaces for each room (made possible by the more extended use of coal) as though the thought of sun and air grows more important. Climate controlled the choice of site, for one too low is associated with damp; and one on the top of a hill too exposed. As a rule there was protection from north and east. It is interesting to follow how the mediaeval moated house left its low-lying ground and in the course of time moved slowly up the hill. The climate, if it is sombre, is also equable, and allows a rich vegetation. English trees are a part of every landscape, every village, and every house and garden. Oaks and elms, beeches, limes, and chestnuts, today grow into more splendid groups and in greater masses here than anywhere else. With trees is coupled turf, for although turf is found abroad even so far south as Italy, it is probably only in England that there exists such rich and everlasting grass, grass that with a little care can be cultured into a carpet more perfect than was ever made by hand. As if in natural contrast to the turf, there are flowers, and here again England has at her disposal a heritage that is open to all.

With all this varied beauty of landscape and materials, it is not surprising that the old English garden has round it a glamour. Perhaps it is the very simplicity of the Englishman that unknowingly has allowed the material to triumph, casting over them all an ingenuousness that is sometimes both so noble and disarming. There is none of that profound thought that enabled the Italian to succeed in spite of his materials, and there is little suggestion of the magnificent sophistication of Le Nôtre. If the Englishman has tried frankly to copy either one or the other, he has almost invariably failed, and the garden, if it is fine, is so in spite of his efforts. The technique behind the English plan is as a rule elementary, and this accounts for the lack of unity in our own gardens in comparison with the work of other countries. One presumes the designer may have studied the plan only on the site, and was thus unable to grasp the whole.

1450-1550

Looking back into the past, one sees how the design of the garden grows out of the Middle Ages, for the thirteenth century in its own way was intellectually England's greatest period. The philosophy of St. Thomas Aquinas and the conception of the west front of Wells Cathedral mean

Eardisland, Herefordshire

thought as profound as any in the world's history. Dating from then, the power of the Church echoes down the ages, with all its mysticism, idealism and narrow ways, superstition and personal discomfort. By the reign of Henry VII its power had so far declined that in conjunction with other influences, such as the invention of gunpowder that rendered obsolete the fortified castle, houses here and there began to rise having round them a garden not enclosed by the high walls of the monastery garden, and containing more freedom than those simple squares suggested. It is significant that although the mediaeval man shut out nature, he was himself more akin to it than in those later days when terraces were built up at enormous cost to survey the landscape as though it were some strange spectacle. On emerging from castle or monastery, itself usually placed in a romantic setting, he unconsciously built a house and garden possibly more related than at any other time to the countryside.

It is in the heart of Gloucestershire, set remotely away in a deep valley of the hills, that perhaps the earliest complete garden is found – Owlpen Manor. No definite date is recorded, but the house goes back to the thirteenth century, was considerably altered under Elizabeth, and again about 1616. At the back of the little group that comprises church and manor, a hill looms dark and tremendous. In front the ground rises less abruptly to another, and on either side more wood-crowned hills gather round the valley. The scheme is scarcely more than half an acre. Today the yews are far beyond the size originally intended, but they cast over the place

Owlpen Manor, Gloucestershire

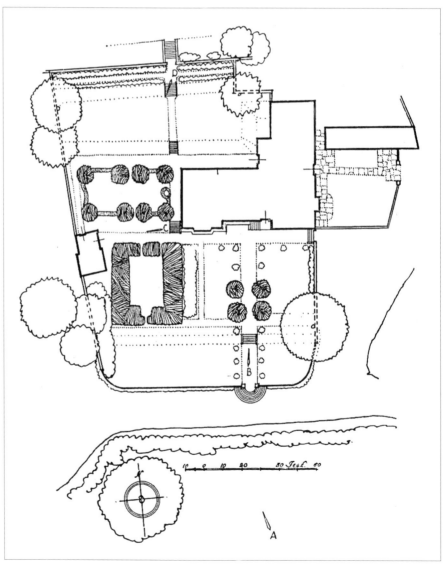

Owlpen Manor

Owlpen Manor, Gloucestershire: Viewpoint A on plan

a gloom and mystery consonant with the superstition of the Middle Ages. Between their cliffs, more important as a mass than the house itself, the ways seem puny and small. The yew parlour is a place where witches brew up mischief. Everything is cramped and narrow. The steps from terrace to terrace are steep and difficult, and there is little personal comfort to be derived from walking about. Over the little garden the church is ever present, symbolic of the power it once held over the souls of the people who lived below; and over the group, let into the garden by glimpses between the yew, hang the ponderous hills more lasting than anything. As a design the garden at Owlpen is admirably planned for its position. For so small an area there is intense interest, and with it all the scale is fine. The main terrace of yews carries the house on to the now almost completely hidden garden house, and it is round this group that the scheme is built; the parlour was never meant to have the importance it has today. If the place is too overwhelming for its size, it suggests how strong is the power of garden magic to transport one back over the centuries.

Owlpen Manor is the last of mediaevalism and the first of individualism. History advanced, and probably about the time when Henry VIII was renouncing the papacy, the garden at Bingham's Melcombe in Dorset was laid out for an older building. The crampedness of the Middle Ages has almost gone, but the unconscious relation to its surroundings remains in the fine if unsophisticated lines of the garden. The group is again situated remotely among hills, but the hills are farther away and lower, ringing themselves round the buildings in a partial amphitheatre. A wide valley leads in the opposite direction. The church is away among trees, out of sight

Owlpen Manor: Viewpoint B on plan

Owlpen Manor: Viewpoint C on plan

Owlpen Manor: Viewpoint D on plan

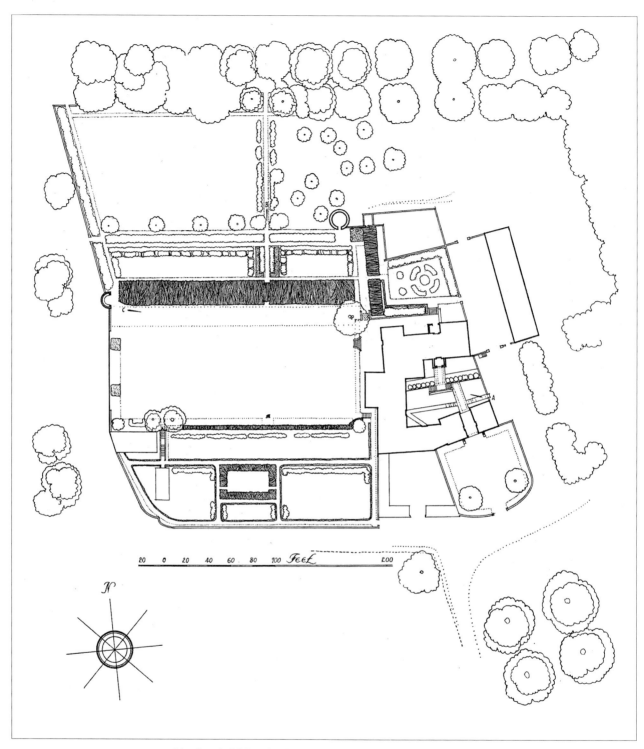

20 0 20 40 60 80 100 *Feet* 200

N

Bingham's Melcombe, Dorset

Bingham's Melcombe, Dorset

of the garden. Though one of the earliest examples of a collection of gardens of more than one type, the real strength of the scheme lies in the breadth of the garden with its slender contrasting axis and its suitability to a haphazard house. The approach leads down the remains of a fine avenue, through a thirteenth-century ghost-haunted gatehouse, and into a courtyard full of odd angles and shapes, one side open over a low parapet wall and in their season hydrangeas on the little terrace throwing over all a glow of colour. Under the porch containing the powder closet one goes through the hall into what is known as the ladies' garden, a small walled enclosure where flowers grow in quiet seclusion before the windows. From here a sunk path skirts the buildings to the west front, where the new garden passing down the gentle slope to the south pauses before the house in the bowling green. To the right a bank supports a colossal yew hedge, in front there would have been a framed view up the valley, and to the left, where the ground drops more steeply to a lower terrace containing the kitchen garden, a broad calm meadow continues up to trees and the hills beyond. Lawn and hedge slumber through the years. From this spaciousness a little path leads through the yew hedge (so old that the trunks and branches inside form a vast impenetrable network, so huge that it has encroached upon and enveloped a terrace that once ran along the bank parallel to the lawn), and thence into a flower and fruit garden, shadowed and protected by the mighty hedge on one side, and partially enclosed by walls or hedges or fruit trees on the others. The paths are admirably arranged to visit the flowers intimately, and at the same time preserve the scale of the rest in the simplicity of their lines. Near one end is that favourite device of the period, a circular dovecot, and in those days the cooing of doves was heard perpetually. Our little path, crossing the flower walk, passes up through the orchard and into a great wooded avenue from which the garden down the hill seems to have started. Along the

Bingham's Melcombe, Dorset: Viewpoint B on plan

Bingham's Melcombe, Dorset: Viewpoint A on plan

Bingham's Melcombe, Dorset: Viewpoint C on plan

Bingham's Melcombe, Dorset. From the meadow

avenue, today leading from nowhere to nowhere in particular, one reaches, almost in the depths of a wood, a little fishpond, where the stream that feeds it comes fresh out of the trees.

1550-1625

Meanwhile the suppression of the monasteries supplied vast wealth to the king and nobles, and was a direct cause of the private building that now began to take place all over the country. One supposes that the meeting of Henry VIII and Francis I on the Field of the Cloth of Gold gave this country the most stimulating impetus to the consideration of personal comfort that it had ever received. Other causes were at work to further the same movement that, as the Renaissance, had been taking place in Italy for over a hundred years. The Wars of the Roses had denuded the land of the flower of mediaeval nobility, and the younger men who took their place were more susceptible to new influences. The rounding of the Horn quickly followed the capture of Constantinople by the Turks, and so opened up trade and circulation in the northern countries in favour of those along the Mediterranean. Caxton introduced printing, and it was about this time that the individual began to travel abroad. The King himself gathered round him a few Italian craftsmen, building Nonsuch Palace, not a trace of which now remains. Wolsey rebuilt Hampton Court with its still enclosed gardens, and among others Layer Marney Towers in Essex, and Sutton Place in Surrey, were great houses, probably with simple gardens, that carry us through the short reign of Edward VI, the turbulent days of Mary, to the reign of Queen Elizabeth.

Reviewing England's position politically and intellectually in those days, it is not surprising that her mansions were as fine in their own way as any contemporary building throughout Europe. The spirit of adventure and the command of the high seas led to the formation of colonies from which accrued wealth and power. In literature and drama a greater collection of names has rarely been gathered together. In architecture and the plastic arts it was a time when the tradition of cathedral building combined with the freshness of the day to absorb and make use of any ideas that might filter through from Italy. Unlike the châteaux of the Loire, there is nothing fanciful about an Elizabethan mansion. It is eminently logical, with an appreciation of mass and form, of planes and shadows that stand out boldly in this atmosphere where the clear-cut shadows under the cornices and mouldings of a classic building exist only for a few days of the year. The architect, as an individual, now began to come into prominence, for with one or two notable exceptions all mediaeval work was done by the community, and the name of the artist rarely appeared. It was a period, too, when the English country gentleman was often sufficiently educated in the arts to undertake, like Lord Salisbury at Hatfield, the design of his own house and gardens. Nor seldom have these places the touch of an amateur, though it is true that more than one house dating from this period depends on age for any beauty it may have. Elizabeth herself must have given great impetus to garden design. She loved the dignity of an avenue, and she loved

Above and below: Cleeve Prior, Evesham. The Twelve Apostles

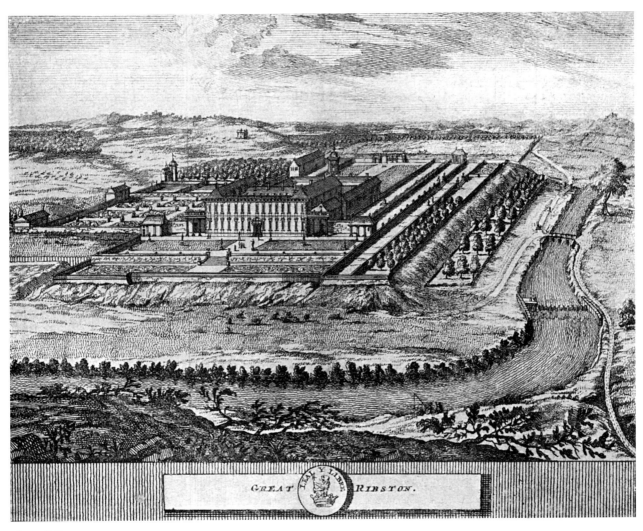

Great Ribston

to visit the country seats of the nobles. A Royal Progress in those days was an affair of importance, and one learns with wonder how a mighty vista was cut in the night at one house at which she rested. Open-air pageants, and entertainments that were often held in the gardens, all helped to give thoughtful consideration to the lay-out. Francis Bacon has described the ideal garden of the period according to his own lights, but, reading between the lines, posterity learns little more than that the garden was profoundly appreciated from the point of view of design, and that the English garden of that date might be getting stereotyped, if it were not for the minor interests it contained. No longer was the country the direct inspiration of the scheme, nor was the interest as yet held by the artificial design of the Renaissance; there was probably a more varied spirit in the smaller manor houses and cottages that sprinkled the countryside, rich in individuality. The typical garden of an Elizabethan mansion was first a definite base to the house, and nothing could be finer than the steady sweep of grass that often lay before the buildings. The rectangular compartments of the garden carried on the bluntness of the building, and in these compartments were very simple pleached alleys and galleries to provide shade; there were arbours, fishponds, topiary work, generally a raised walk from which to see the view or garden, and sometimes a mount. The garden house, carrying on

Poxwell, Dorset. Gatehouse

Beckington, Somerset. Garden house

the architecture, appears constantly. All these had been expanded from ideas in the Middle Ages, but the mound, at any rate, suggests how detached the Elizabethan was becoming from his surroundings; in the enclosed garden of the Middle Ages it was at least a necessity. At this time, just as with the detail on the buildings, the worse side of the Italian influence was beginning to be felt in such conceits as water-works and grottos, details that were not so well absorbed by the spirit of the garden as they had been by that of the house. The heart of the garden lay in the still mediaeval flowers and knots. Flowers were planted in square beds, raised above the surrounding paths. A knot was a more intricate design than a flower bed, and its interest therefore lay in the form of the pattern rather than the colours. These were made up of rosemary, hyssop, and thyme, and soon developed so that the borders were to be of " 'Roses, thorns, lavendar, rosemaries, isop, sage, and such like,' and filled in with primroses and violets, 'Daffydown dillies,' 'sweet Sissely,' 'go to bed at noone,' and all sweet flowers, but chief of all with gilly flowers, the favourite flower of the English Renaissance."*

There is, perhaps, no complete Elizabethan or early Stuart garden today, although many houses still exist to tell of the greatness of that age. Many of them have preserved a certain character, and Montacute in Somersetshire gives a suggestion of the house in relation to its surroundings. The ornaments pricking the sky show how the Elizabethan was still feeling the influence of the now distant mediaevalism. Two great houses, both belonging to the Earl of Salisbury, and dating from the time of James I, are still Elizabethan in character. Cranborne Manor in Dorset was used mainly as a hunting lodge, and the enclosed forecourt to the south and enclosed garden to the north may date from an earlier time than when Viscount Cranborne, later the first Earl of Salisbury, turned the house from a fortified manor into an up-to-date residence. There is all the suggestion of the love of open air in the loggia, its details and idea clearly taken from Italy, even to the aspect, but ably worked into traditional architecture. Hatfield House was a grander undertaking. The house is placed on the highest ground, and is definitely the centre of a lay-out that stretches symmetrically from each façade. To the north there is the approach avenue and forecourt, to the east a series of open descending terraces, to the south another but more spacious grass avenue framed in between twin garden houses, and to the west are gardens more secluded. Here is the square flower garden with its enclosing foliaged gallery reminiscent of Bacon's garden.

1625-1700

The accession of Charles I to the throne in 1625 meant the introduction of the Renaissance with its full significance. That monarch was both powerful and interested enough to further the arts in England personally, and Inigo Jones was the great personality at hand. It was from his wide travels in Italy that Inigo Jones felt the stirrings that the Italian nation had felt two hundred years before. He brought back to his native country a discipline in architecture to find the counterpart of which one has to go back as far as

* Reginald Blomfield, 'The Formal Garden in England'; William Lawson, 'The Countrie Housewife's Garden' (1618)

Cranborne Manor, Dorset

Cranborne Manor, Dorset.
Gatehouse

126

Montacute, Somerset

Roman days. A firm hold was laid upon houses and gardens up and down the country, modified only slightly to conform to climatic and other conditions. In the hands of Inigo Jones or, after the fire of London, Christopher Wren, these notions from abroad were moulded into a very fine architecture, but in smaller hands gardens especially were liable to suffer from the misguided copying of foreign examples. One wonders to what an extent that gifted amateur, John Evelyn, who visited and described so many gardens in Italy at that period, influenced the Englishman by the letter rather than the spirit of the Italian garden. But many fine houses, built of English materials and still with the traditional idea of compartments lurking behind their design, date from this time. Two huge walled gardens, the enormous built-up view terrace, and, above all, the piers, are all that remain of Hamstead Marshall in Berkshire. The conception is of the simplest, for it was but an enlargement of the earlier gardens. The site is a level piece of high ground, with views around. The garden has taken a certain area, and planted itself quite crudely on the ground, but the terrace is there for anyone who takes the trouble to climb up and see the view. Despite the bluntness of placing, now very much softened by time, these places had a simple dignity that earlier or later gardens with their sympathy or technique must often have lacked. There is charm especially over the small English house and garden, broadly termed Georgian, that is largely due to the fine proportion of the one and the simplicity of the other. In detail, many sophisticated foreign examples were often well employed to adorn traditional buildings. The course that garden planning took in England before the French influence stepped in is represented to us today

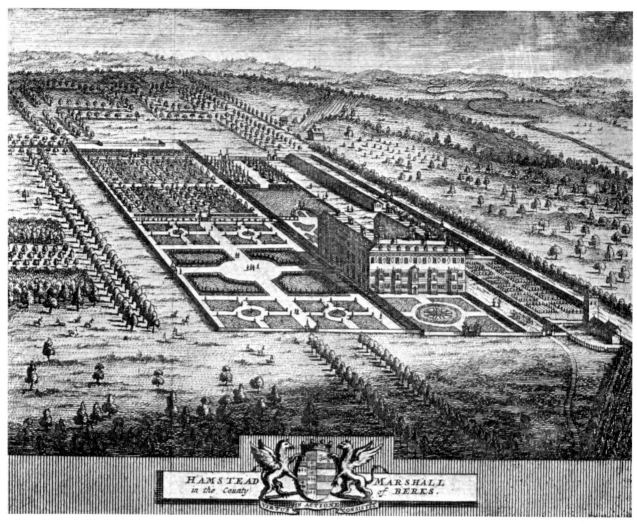

Hamstead Marshall, Berkshire

mainly by the many prints that were made at the time. The knowledge of planning, apart from the house, that first came over with the Renaissance, was particularly slight. At the time Wren may be said to be almost the only one with any technique at all. When the site chosen seemed more interesting than at Hamstead Marshall, the gardens were extended on traditional rectangular lines to any extent, sometimes, even so late as at New Park in Surrey, making enormous excavations to make their terraces. Other gardens, like Ragly in Warwickshire, betrayed a technique in formal planning that must have been almost disheartening in its perfect symmetry. While these undoubtedly stately and well-proportioned houses were setting themselves down bluntly in some of the choicest scenery in England, alterations were being made to many older existing houses in bringing them up to date. Because these places were older and generally smaller than those of the day, the English tradition behind them was still strong enough to absorb and make use of fresh ideas, much as the Elizabethan mansion had done many years before. Over Packwood in Warwickshire and Canons Ashby in Northamptonshire there still lingers the spell of the house and garden that belong to the country in which they have grown.

Warwickshire has a large share of associations peculiarly English: Kenilworth Castle, Compton Wynyates (the most intriguing of all mediaeval

Hamstead Marshall, Berkshire

Charlton Horethorne, Dorset

Above: At Climping, Sussex
Below: Percy Lodge, Richmond
Typical late Renaissance houses

The Flower Garden at Hatfield House

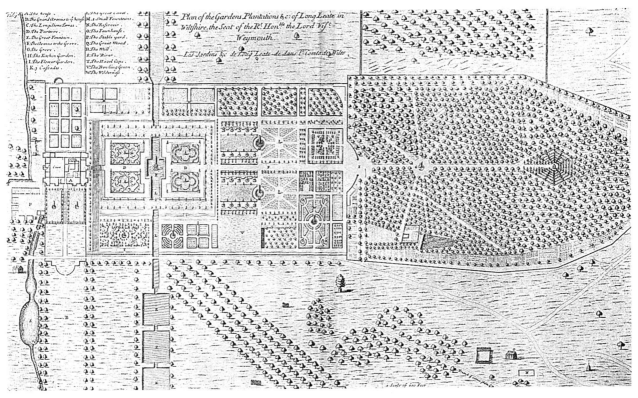

Longleat, Wiltshire. (By London and Wise)

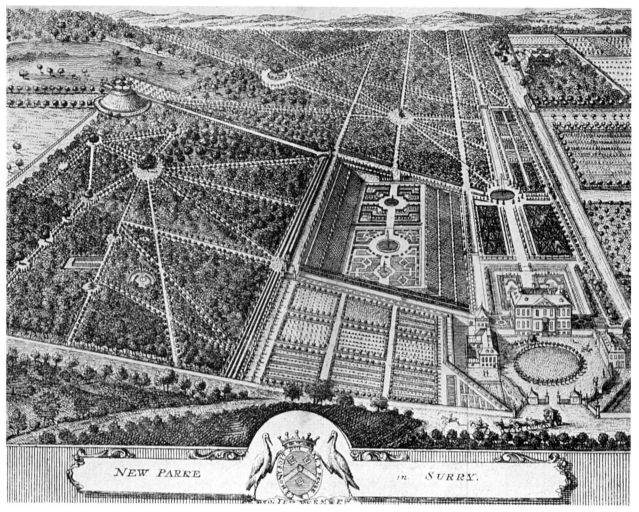

New Park, Surrey

houses), and finally Stratford-on-Avon and the Forest of Arden. It is a few miles north of the long straggling town of Henley-in-Arden that one discovers one of the most curious gardens in the country. Packwood is essentially English. It has that want of a complete unified plan (for the group of buildings that embrace the road are the result of accident as much as design) that seems to characterise English work; it plays with the most beautiful materials; and, above all, it has a worldliness combined with a curious vague, indefinable mysticism that seems to be somehow inherent in the northern race. The garden mainly lies south-east of the house, and is a direct throw-back to earlier days. It is entered from the house or by a door in the wall from the forecourt, and from that moment, owing to the slight stage-like rise in the ground, the whole garden lies outstretched. In the foreground is the rectangular flower garden, its corners once enclosing four little garden houses. The small raised terrace so reminiscent of earlier days separates this from what lies behind: yews and mysticism. It is the story of the Sermon on the Mount. Step into this medley and its idea takes us back to the days when the teaching of the Church held its sway over the human mind. The lawyer who planted these yews must have been a disciple of Milton.

When we pass up the central way we are passing through the strange

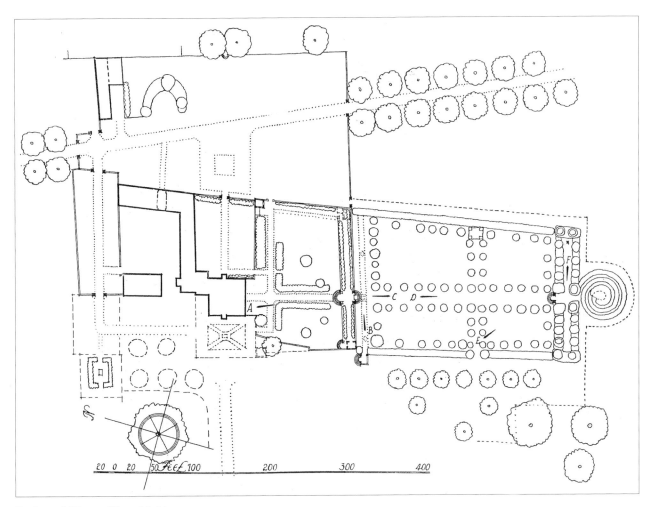

Packwood House, Warwickshire

Packwood House, Warwickshire: Viewpoint A on plan

Packwood House, Warwickshire: Viewpoint D on plan

Packwood House, Warwickshire: Viewpoint E on plan

Packwood House, Warwickshire: Viewpoint F on plan

Packwood House, Warwickshire: Viewpoint C on plan

Packwood House, Warwickshire: Viewpoint B on plan

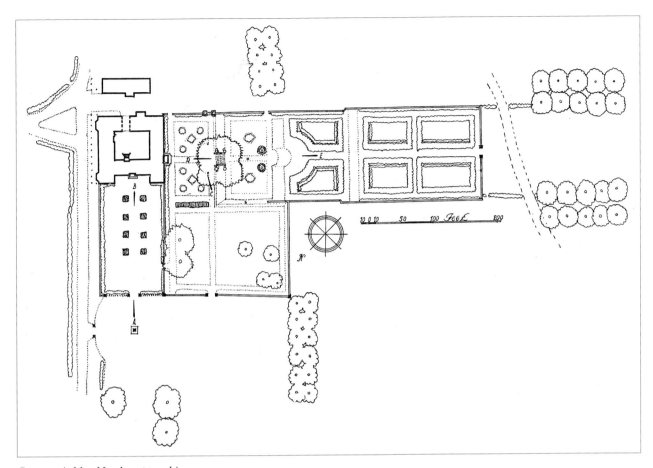

Canons Ashby, Northamptonshire

diverse shapes of the multitude; at the top are the twelve apostles with the four evangelists in the centre; and on the Mount is the tree symbolising the Teacher. Reached by a spiral path after such an impressive journey, the arbour in the tree must have been, and remains, a place for deepest meditation. Over the garden there would have been heard the buzzing of the bees whose hives were contained in the holes of the terrace wall; the orchard along the west boundary brings us back to today; and the great elms remind us of the freshness of country that lies beyond.

Canons Ashby is situated in an undulating and fairly well-wooded part of Northamptonshire, and together with the church and one or two cottages makes a harmonious group of warm brown stone. The house dates back from the fortified times of the small enclosed courtyard and battlemented tower, but its subsequent history is written more clearly in the garden. The approach, disused today, leads up to a partially enclosed forecourt, and Renaissance piers and details contrast in age and design with the older work. Out into the garden a vista stretches between two splendid cedars, two clipped trees that yield to the lines of the cedars, two more gate piers, a double row of elms, and so on into infinity. This is the central part of the garden, but to one side is another simpler grass square, again open to the south, but with an entirely different prospect from that given by the avenue. There is nothing but a four-foot drop between the built-up ground of the terrace and a broad meadow that goes sweeping down to a lake and up and over the hill beyond. There are many small details in the garden that help to give it the quality of permanence. There is the remains of a stately avenue

Canons Ashby, Northamptonshire

Canons Ashby, Northamptonshire: Viewpoint A on plan

Canons Ashby, Northamptonshire: Viewpoint D on plan

Canons Ashby, Northamptonshire: Viewpoint B on plan

Canons Ashby,
Northamptonshire:
Viewpoint E on plan

The Canal at Hampton
Court

Canons Ashby, Northamptonshire: Viewpoint C on plan

of trees; the church is far enough away not to be oppressive, but its tower has become an integral part of the garden; terraces give an unexpected variety and substance to the buildings. The lay-out is so simple and open it carries us back to earlier days, and although such history as is available seems against us, we can imagine that the parts of the garden extending from the two façades entirely date from 1550 rather than only a portion. In 1708 Sir Edward Dryden came to alter the house and add the fancy to relieve the severe. Later the English School of Landscape Gardening must have been responsible not only for the cedars that give so much of the character, but probably also for arranging the view towards the lake into a definite pictorial composition.

WILLIAM AND MARY

These two, Packwood and Canons Ashby, though comparatively late in date, were unaffected by the Restoration and the consequences that followed on the close relations between Charles Stuart and France. France was now at the height of her prestige and glory. All Europe was turning to her for inspiration in the arts, for Louis set the fashion for the world. It became acknowledged that a magnificent house demanded a magnificent garden. The elements that go to make a French garden, avenues and canals, were seized upon and used profusely in English gardens. At Hampton Court, London and Wise laid out the semicircular garden before Wren's buildings, and planted the radiating avenues with the canal in the central, perhaps the first of its kind in England. Wrest in Bedfordshire was another great scheme with one central canal leading up to a monumental pavilion by Archer. Le Nôtre himself undoubtedly came over, and among other designs attributed to him was almost certainly responsible for the Mall. With the grand ideas

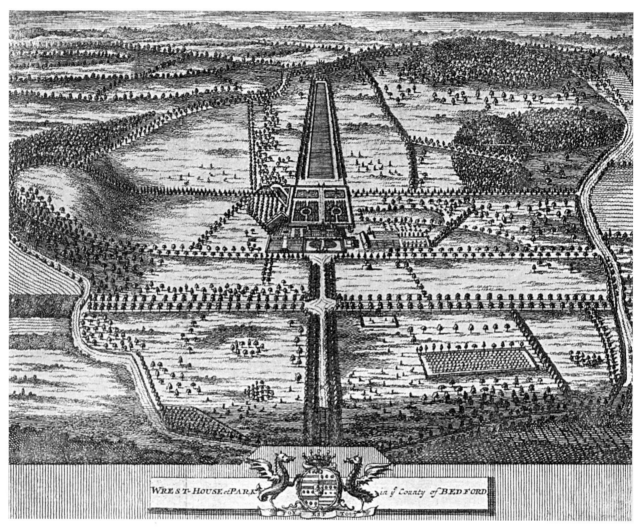

Wrest House, Bedfordshire

came also details that the French had brought to such perfection – box parterre with its rich shapes, "charmilles," cascades and sculpture.

In 1688, however, William and Mary secured the English throne. With them came a host of partisans, and there spread through the country an influence of the Netherlands that for a brief space broke in upon that of France. We must turn to the low-lying flats and canals of Holland to see how garden architecture had been developing in that country. The cultivation of flowers, especially tulips, had the first consideration, and the garden was often a studied and firm architectural background to flowers. So rises the term "Dutch garden" that became popular in England at this period. The small space available, and the difficulty of growing large trees owing to the soil and wind, led also to a violent development of topiary work, and we can suppose that Anne was not altogether unjustified in removing the overgrown semicircular parterre topiary garden at Hampton Court. Perhaps because of the confined spaces, the Dutchman loved to contemplate the passing world over his pipe, and it is in that country that the clairvoyée and the gazebo are in their natural element. The clairvoyée is the broad window in the walls of an enclosed garden, and the gazebo at that time was a small pavilion each of whose windows might give a different prospect; one especially looked upon the high-road and the approach. Above all, the Dutch influence on garden

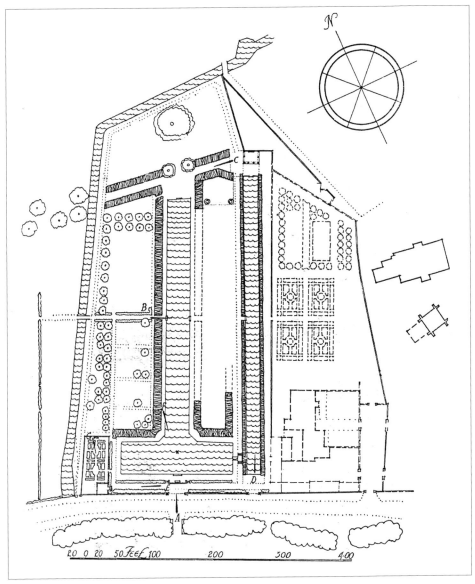

Westbury-on-Severn, Gloucestershire. Showing conjectural plan of original house

design brought over with it a calm, comfort-loving point of view reminiscent of the substantial wealthy traders of Amsterdam.

On the further side of the Severn estuary, where a plain separates the river from the forest-crowned hills and mountains of Wales, and in striking contrast both in situation and character to the not far distant Owlpen Manor, lies a garden built by a partisan of William III, having in its design the combined qualities of Englishman and Dutchman. The church tower and spire at Westbury are unique in the country, and it may have been this thirteenth-century free standing feature, so markedly vertical, that inspired the long low lines of the garden itself. Once it was definitely a part of the scheme, but its place as a foil is taken today by the twin poplars that herald the end of the T-canal. The main Roman road to the village passes one of two gazebos, its window now blocked up, and in a moment piers announce a clairvoyée in the wall. After the road outside nothing could be so refreshing to the passer-by as this garden spread so generously before him: the canal, grass perpetually emerald because of its position, dark green

Westbury-on-Severn, Gloucestershire: Viewpoint A on plan

Westbury-on-Severn, Gloucestershire: Viewpoint B on plan

Westbury-on-Severn, Gloucestershire: Viewpoint F on plan

Westbury-on-Severn, Gloucestershire: Viewpoint E on plan

Westbury-on-Severn, Gloucestershire: Viewpoint D on plan

Westbury-on-Severn, Gloucestershire: Viewpoint G on plan

Westbury-on-Severn, Gloucestershire: Viewpoint C on plan

hedges, and to one side the garden house rising straight above the hedges, with the warm red brick and white windows contrasting with the rest. Farther on there is another clairvoyée and a small canal leads directly to the little house. Within the garden itself all is peaceful. The mansion and the parterre garden in front of it have gone, and probably many of the hedges may have been topiary. Only once, apart from the clairvoyée, has it been necessary to take us out of this garden. One avenue leads from that viewpoint, the garden house, skewed round to lead the eye along what was once an avenue of pear trees over the top of an unusually undulating piece of ground. Leaving the elevated room of the garden house, so carefully considered from its main proportions, a perfect cube, to the smallest mouldings, and passing through what is left of the quincunx, the orchard, we come to the head of the T-canal, and entering the gateway by the gazebo, discover a small intimate rose garden, two windows looking upon it. Westbury is always calm and thoughtful, unruffled when the clouds in the canal are chasing those in the sky, but calmer when the sun sends across the long shadows of the poplars or the tip of the ancient spire reaches the water.

ANNE

The French wars under Queen Anne soon caused the Dutch influence to decline, and even before the treaty of Utrecht houses and gardens were begun more than ever French in character. Among them is Bramham Park in Yorkshire, created by the well-travelled Lord Bingley in 1712. A vast tract of country is brought into the scheme, not merely the hundred or so acres that immediately adjoin the house, but several thousand that surround this again. The map suggests the extent. A gigantic vista stretches across the garden front of the house, finishing to the west on the chapel, and disappearing into the east between charmilles and branching trees, over pools and cascades, across an open stretch of country along a line suggested today by a few beech trees, another wood, a temple, and culminating in an obelisk pricking the distant sky like a needle. Around this far point one knows there is a system of radiating and circular avenues cut through the woods, that suggest a second though less sophisticated lay-out than that by the house. Across this vista a wide important axis descends the hill east of the house, and this, whether so placed because of the lie of the land or not, is in reality the link between the nearer and the distant parks. Round this scheme of house, vista, and cross axis, the paths and interests that constitute the inner park are more or less arranged on a pattern. The house is one of the finest in the country. For all its details that come from Italy, it is a true English mansion, a rugged counterpart of the Yorkshire stone of which it is made. The parts of the garden immediately by the house have been altered except for the lines of the sunk garden, the vista, and the breath of open spaces that is admitted through the short open colonnade on either side of the house. Following the path that leads up past the chapel, across an avenue that gives the first glimpse of the country to the west, one plunges in between towering charmilles, reminiscent of France, enters an open-air diamond-shaped "salon" with passages leading invitingly into the trees,

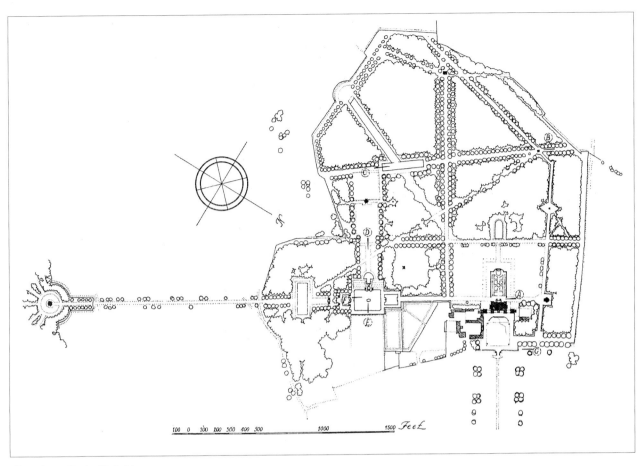

Bramham Park, Yorkshire

continues restfully and all unsuspecting until the path suddenly turns, and there is one of those dramatic views that abound everywhere. In the foreground is the vase of the four faces, from which radiate other avenues, and behind, a noble avenue of trees soaring upwards and arching overhead hurry away to frame a glorious view of distant woods. Along this one proceeds, with the view widening out at every step, and arrives on to what may almost be described as the ramparts. Here can now be seen how firmly the inner park is separated from the country, and yet how generously each extends into the other. The broad walk that encircles nearly half of the park is built up on an average of about six feet above the outside country. The way follows this wall until it reaches a bastion that marks the point where the tail of the T-canal is trying to bring the country to the house. This curious romantic sheet of water was probably an addition to its cross piece. The avenue in which it is set, and the diagonal avenue nearer the house, disturb the simplicity of the rest. Down the canal, mirroring the slender tree trunks, and passing the head with the distant vase of the four faces silhouetted to the west, one arrives at the top of the main cross axis. Past the little Gothic summerhouse that came in later days, there lies outstretched to the north another invitation to the country, more open than the avenues. The square pool lies like a silver streak in its raised position, and beyond this and framed by firm lines the country extends as a background. The cascades that descend on three sides of the pool recall those that descend the hill in the park at St. Cloud, and today the sound that once occurred must be imagined, the culmination in interest and design to the whole scheme.

Bramham Park, Yorkshire: Viewpoint A on plan

Bramham Park, Yorkshire: Viewpoint E on plan

Bramham Park, Yorkshire: Viewpoint B on plan

Bramham Park, Yorkshire: Viewpoint C on plan

*Bramham Park, Yorkshire:
Viewpoint F on plan*

*Bramham Park, Yorkshire:
Viewpoint G on plan*

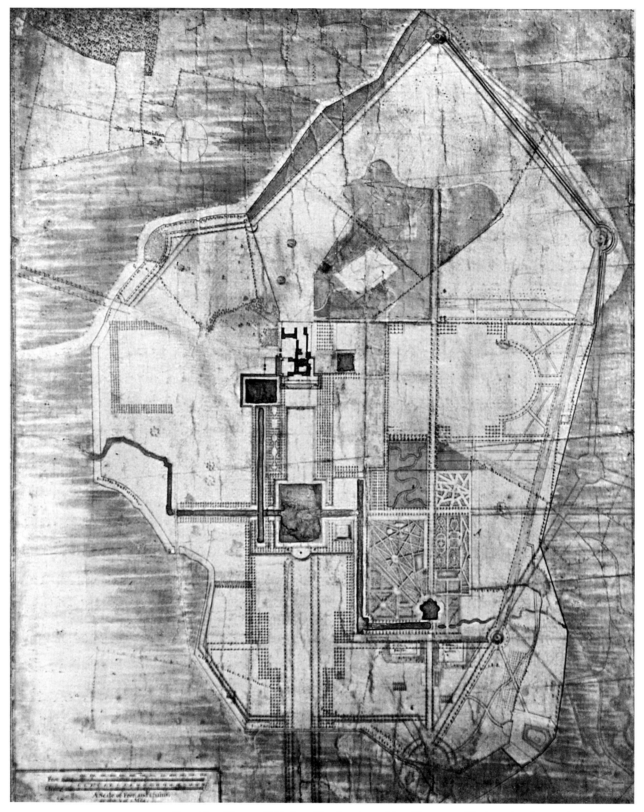

Boughton House, Kettering, Northamptonshire. From an old plan showing projected extensions

Boughton House, Kettering, Northamptonshire. The Centre Way

Boughton House, Kettering, Northamptonshire. One of the avenues

A little later in point of date a finer garden plan, but not so fine a house, was undertaken at Boughton, near Kettering in Northamptonshire. Lord Montague was the English ambassador in France, and was therefore associated with the great gardens there even more than was Lord Bingley; so much so that the grander additions he intended to give the older house were entirely French. The park is French only in its play of masses of trees and canals; in its simple lines and proportions it is very much more English than Bramham. The story goes that Lord Montague, ostensibly in order to give employment after the French wars, wished to plant an avenue the whole seventy-five miles to London. The project could not be realised, and he then planted avenues totalling that distance either across or round his estate. There are some twenty miles of these standing today, and long before the park itself is reached they can be seen like giant feelers

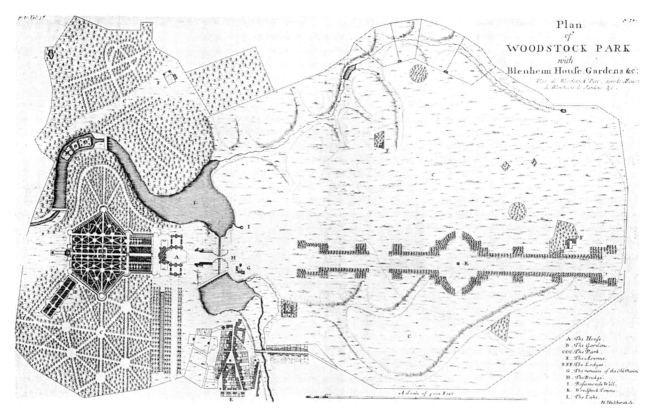

Blenheim Palace, Oxford. From Vitruvius Britannicus

extending from the house up hill and down dale. The park itself, like those of Le Nôtre, is a composition of trees and water, but today the effect has largely to be imagined, for the water has been more or less drained and the trees are imperfect. The grouping of trees down the central way must be as finely and spaciously proportioned as any of the kind in England. It is round this sumptuous way that the interests of water and trees on either side weave themselves into a balance. Vistas that were high and narrow at Bramham have been broadened, from the stretch of grass that continues the central axis over the opposite ridge, to the avenues of elms that choose for effect the most undulating piece of ground. The earthworks, digging canals, making up terraces, and above all the huge mount, were an immense undertaking; they have about them, however, a spirit that is particularly integral with the ground they have modelled. We have seen how in other gardens of this size, such as New Park in Surrey, the ground was treated almost with contempt, great pieces carved out of hillsides with little real relation to the contours. At Boughton it is the undulating ground that has given the inspiration for its modelling, just as the river Ise running through the meadows gave the spirit of the canals.

PALLADIANISM

The beginning of the eighteenth century saw the introduction into this country of Palladianism. Palladio was essentially at home in towns, in Venice or Vicenza, erecting finely proportioned buildings founded on classic severity. When, however, he carried architecture into the plains or along the banks of the Brenta, he carried the same imposing ideas into the country house. These great villas were considered but slightly in relation to their

The Approach to Stowe

position, and the lay-outs round them, if any at all, are mostly of the crudest. Partly because of the prominence that that district had come into in its relations with England, and partly because the severity and dignity of the buildings appealed to the English, it became the fashion in this country to build in the Palladian manner. Just as Wren had absorbed the foreign influence and reproduced it stamped with his own personality, so Sir John Vanbrugh, playwright and architect, appreciated the fundamental sense of design behind Palladio. The palaces of Castle Howard and Blenheim are vast, monstrous, worthy of the scathing satire of Pope, but nevertheless they are, especially the latter, superb specimens of architecture. In the design of the park surrounding Blenheim, Vanbrugh far exceeded both in design and conception any scheme of Palladio, for here is a plan worthy of one of the grandest palaces in England. In honour of the first Duke of Marlborough, for whom the palace was built and only partly paid for by a grateful country, the trees in the avenue are supposed to have been planted in the formation of the Battle of Blenheim. Very shortly afterwards the Landscape School took in hand the surroundings of the great mansions. The approach to Stowe is the threshold of a new world.

CHARACTER

The charm of the old English garden is due to the handling of materials and country rather than to abstract design. In this fact lies the real value of their study. English history shows that in planning either man or country has dominated. In the Renaissance it was frankly the former. In the Middle Ages it was country, for the apparently haphazard grouping of towns, villages and buildings is closely related to nature; Compton Wynyates in Warwickshire might indeed be some strange natural product. Probably the true spirit of England lies somewhere between the two extremes.

PART 3

I

THE ENGLISH SCHOOL
OF LANDSCAPE GARDENING

The arch at Stowe heralds a new era, for by the eighteenth century classicism had run its course, and England began to revolt against what was now crudely a foreign invasion. Huge masses of buildings, many of them fine compositions in themselves, slumbered like giants in a country where people, climate, and landscape were against them. All Europe followed suit. In France, Marie Antoinette escaped from the gardens at Versailles, building herself the hamlet in the gardens of the Petit Trianon. In England Pope poured ridicule on both the grandeur that classicism had reached and the conceits to which it had fallen. Of Blenheim he wrote: "'Tis very fine, but where d'ye sleep and where d'ye dine?" and at an imaginary sale of clipped evergreens, "a quickset hog, shot up into a porcupine, by its being forgot a week in rainy weather." The cry was for the return to the Gothic age, the true tradition of England; and the loudest answer came from Horace Walpole's Strawberry Hill. Everywhere romance coloured the arts. At first it was declared that garden architecture as such must cease to exist. Walpole, speaking of William Kent, the first landscape architect, says: "Kent leapt the fence and saw that all nature was a garden." The hard lines of architecture were to be removed as much as possible, and nature brought to the threshold of the house. Paths were made to curl and curve, for nature has no straight line. At that date England set the fashion for the world, and the wholesale destruction of older gardens that took place extended as far as Italy. For a time the sense of association held the field without a rival. Quaint things associated with nature or mediaevalism were introduced for their own sake. Because ruins had about them the glamour of romance, imitation ruins of Gothic buildings or Grecian temples were scattered about the grounds. Capability Brown probably marks the climax of romanticism, erecting church steeples to enhance the interest of a view. Under his direction vast areas of countryside were altered and "improved". At Blenheim he constructed the artificial lake, the sight of which, when completed, caused him to cry: "Thames, Thames, wilt thou ever forgive me?" Underlying Brown's work, however, there is a keen sense of design, and among his many followers there is one, Humphrey Repton, who did not hesitate to condemn faults of his predecessors. Though this period never produced a single really great man to bring landscape design to its ultimate stage, yet Repton was an artist with the ability to consider the whole of his subject in an unbiased way. He saw that nature was a garden of itself alone, that it cannot be copied, and that the principles of landscape design are the same as those of any design. In reality, landscape gardens are possibly more artificial than the older gardens that precede them. The former in principle absorb the country, while the latter are absorbed by it.

The lasting monument of the English Landscape School is the park. The period found the aristocracy prouder and wealthier than ever, and a stately home was as much a hallmark of dignity as a line of ancestors. Everything that suggested work in any form was kept out of sight; round the house was gathered all that was noblest in the countryside.

The park can be conceived as an introduction between the house and a surrounding country in its virgin state, where forests and bald plains contrast, and where there are no hedges nor villages to break up the land into a smaller scale. All art is in a sense illusion; the mind can wander farther than the eye. In a truly English park, where expanse of turf sweeps between groups of trees and over the tops of hills into infinity, greater spaces still are suggested to the imagination. The extent varies to which the mind is thus allowed to wander, but undoubtedly the imagination at this period was fresh from its long confinement under classicism. Formality had been overstressed, and the repose of an avenue where the eye is firmly directed on its course gave way to arrangement that was stimulating rather than restful. For a time the landscape architect followed the landscape painter. Such artists as Claude were studied both for massing of light and shade and the countless little interesting things that go to make a single view. Here the likeness to the sister art ceases. The spectator in a park moves about, and the effect round him is constantly changing. Carefully arranged pictorial compositions from the house or from particular points in the park are not in themselves sufficient to make a design. If the plan is as carefully composed as any classic plan, groups of trees, and water, fall naturally into pleasant arrangement from whatever view they are seen.

To the early pioneers of the return to nature, the house proved a stumbling-block. If the house was ignored as an unfortunate necessity for man, there still remained such considerations as the approach. Turf drives proved inadequate, and gravel covered in moss too slippery. The things that civilisation demands may be trivial, but they are essential. Brown admitted a "line of formality" between house and park. It was Repton who first seriously appreciated the incongruity, and began slowly to build house and park together. Oriental influence was now pronounced in England, and the traditional Japanese garden in its relation to house has a bearing on the ideal of the Landscape School. In Japan the garden is a landscape formalised, and the house itself is but a further stage from this. Types of rooms inside are not only expressed in its arrangement, but every room has a similar aspect. This produces a building that to Western minds is quaintly informal and straggly; in reality, house and garden are a perfect blend. In England, though the true spirit of Oriental informality was left behind in Japan, Repton began to break up the great block of the house into shadows and planes, "designing," as he says, "in the Gothic manner". Actually he was feeling his way to the traditional forms that had grown up through the influence of English landscape. There is already in a house of this character an element of nature. Between house and park were one or two terraces, the last with a scarcely visible line between the mown grass of the one and the rough turf of the other. The subtlest introduction lies in the planting of trees, composing in formal groups immediately by the house, and widening outwards in groups of trees and copses that grow less pronouncedly arranged as they recede. Outposts of the house appeared in scattered lodges or summer-houses, spreading abroad its character and materials.

162

Stowe

The Lake at Blenheim

Malvern Hall. (By Constable.)

Because the scale of a house and park is so great that any open introduction between the two in the way of a garden cannot be intimate, the flower garden was hidden away in a walled enclosure, which itself became an element in the massing of the house.

Only for a brief period was nature literally brought to the door. Soon the need of an introduction between house and country began once more to be felt, and the park unconsciously answered the need. The relation to the country is illusory, because the surroundings are nearly always imagined. On the one hand no visible boundaries were to enclose the park, whose

Prior Park, Bath

extent was limitless; on the other, the surrounding country in England is nearly always agricultural and therefore broken up into fields. The traditional countryside had either to be seen from a distance, or so altered in character as to be in harmony with the park. Compare such apparently contrasting types as the gardens of Versailles to Arundel Park, in the immediate relation to their surroundings. Both pass out into humbler surroundings, the one by dominating avenues, the other boldly by suggestion; only when the country is grander is it admitted, Versailles being open to the Satory Woods across the Swiss Lake, and Arundel to the South Downs. The admission of the planes of a distant view is one of the noblest attributes of the park, for the simple foreground offers no rivalry in interest. The relation of the design to its immediate site is equally integral. More often than not the site extends over hills and valleys, and the curving shapes of rich deciduous trees echo the rolling lines on which they stand.

The elimination of most of nature's interests is the first step towards unity as it is to a broad effect. The principal elements in a park, apart from the house or lake, are turf and trees, and the whole scheme might almost be regarded as being modelled in a solid green material. Nature deftly plays her variations afterwards. Trees are marshalled into groups, and the groups are arranged about the ground, balancing each other asymmetrically in size, shape, and position. Deer scattered here and there not only carry on an association of ideas, but give to trees what is called a "browsing line". Every tree is brought into uniformity with its neighbours by this base line, where foliage ceases six feet from the ground.

The art of perspective was developed under the influence of painting, and was at times carried to extremes. The art lies in deceiving the eye to a certain extent, and no more; beyond this the sensibility revolts. A broad river is certainly finer in a park than a narrow lake, but when the two ends of the river are seen to be dummies, a favourite device, the illusion once broken cannot be mended. On the other hand, if a view is increased in distance by the closing in of receding groups of trees, the subtlety never

Baths of Apollo, Versailles

obtrudes. The appreciation of size in the distance is difficult without any work of man, from architectural features to ploughed fields, to give scale, and often relies upon the deer, whose size is known and constant. The eye is as easily misled by suggestion. A house that stands low in a valley acquires both a sense of dryness and dignity if there is a lake even only a few feet below it. The eye leaps to the lightest point in the view, the surface of water, and from that level judges the relative height of things around. The initial problem of the approach is solved by perspective: a direct one over undulating ground both conforms to the general roundness of things and heralds the house across the park. When water is introduced into the picture its brightness instantly attracts the eye, and can alter the character of a view. At Lathom, the character of a framed view of a grove of oaks was given by a formal pool across which it was seen as a secondary interest. To make the interest return to the distance, the pool was removed.

The English Landscape School was associated with a host of trouble that did not cease when ruins lost their fashion. People who misunderstood the principles brought down upon it by their work a discredit it did not deserve. Without the sense of design that underlies the composition of rocks at Versailles such ideas of nature come to grief. Contemporary architecture was deplorable, and the house was seldom worthy of the park in which it was set. The park itself carries with it a sense of fresh clean air and glorious spaces, worthy of the country.

II

LITTLE THAKEHAM, SUSSEX

The weald of Sussex, protected on the north and south by downs, is like a chessboard, every field coloured by its own cultivation. Across this the roads from London to the south coast towns thread their way, linking together the towns and villages they pass. The downs come prominently into view on the south side of Horsham, and then it is their presence is perpetually felt. Myths and legends crowd round them as thick as the clouds that blow in from the sea: of how a young king of Sussex kept vigil up in Chanctonbury Ring, immersing his head at midnight in the dewpond; or of how Proud Rosalind lived at Amberley Castle.* All day long when the sun is shining they cast shadows upon the busy workaday country that runs up to their base. Little Thakeham stands a long way back from the shadows, and from thereabouts the great rolling spurs can be seen following one another into the distance east and west. The house faces south, and is placed on a small ridge that slopes away gently in front, but drops abruptly to the north to give a view back across the weald. The first impression is one of gables and chimneys rising from surrounding orchards. In the summer the sun warms the tiled roofs and stone walls, but the small windows and massive chimneys tell of its exposed situation, and of the comfort that lies within during a bleak English winter.

Apart from the contours, the main natural features round which the garden was worked were a row of elms that run north and south, a simple belt of trees where the ground begins to rise again to the south, and a break

Eleanor Farjeon, 'Martin Pippin in the Apple Orchard'

Little Thakeham, Sussex

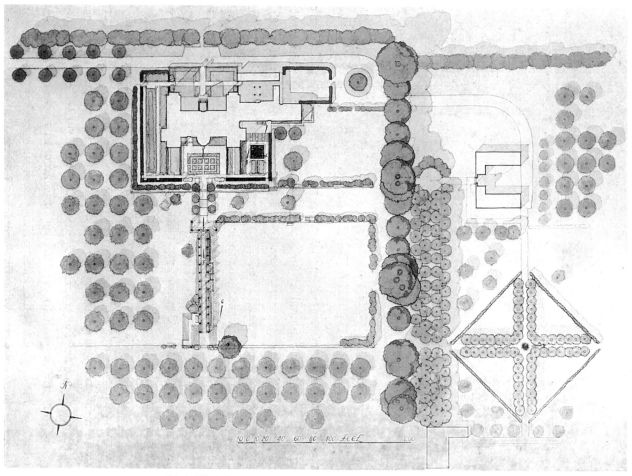

Little Thakeham

to the south-west in this middle distance, that reveals a spur of down dark against the sky. The approach drive from the west leads on past the house to a turning space that is out of sight, and on through the elms to the stables, which with the kitchen garden are thus carefully screened. The house is more or less symmetrical, except for the wing that extends on the east side, and the centre on the garden façade is marked by a great oriel. From this the central axis is carried south between hedges, down a short stepped ramp, on through a pergola built up high above the surrounding land, and so over the intervening orchard to the belt of trees beyond. Otherwise the parts round the house are secluded and made intimate by a formal hedge. Each bay of the house finds its echo on the ground before it. There is the lily pond with its intricacies of rills and steps, from the top of which on most days the down can be seen rolling above the excitement that lies at one's feet. Beside this is a garden of climbing roses; centrally is a stone-paved patterned flower garden; then another like the one before; and finally a garden of peonies and anchusas extending down the side of the house, that was intended to have been finished on a loggia by the entrance. Cut out of the surrounding hedges are alcoves with more seats.

The principal way out of this chaos of flowers and formal architecture, the central walk, leads across a short terrace to the entrance to the pergola. To the left of this a device of steps leads down to the lawn. The east side of the pergola facing the lawn is closed down except for the three central bays, but the whole of the opposite side is open across orchards to that distant

Little Thakeham: Viewpoint A on plan

Little Thakeham: Viewpoint B on plan

Little Thakeham: Viewpoint C on plan

Little Thakeham: Viewpoint D on plan

Little Thakeham: Viewpoint E on plan

glimpse of down, and as if to emphasize the view still more, a monumental flight of steps turns the interest at the end of the walk in that direction. It is delightful to walk down this pergola, so much above the surrounding level and yet with so much sense of protection, roses clambering over the massive cross-pieces, sea pinks lining the path and nestling at the foot of piers. Here the south-west wind blows briskly from the sea. Below, the orchards with their standard planting disappear away on all sides. The great lawn that stretches east of the pergola is a foil to the excitement everywhere else, and from here can be seen how the long line of pergola carries across the firmness of the house into the skyline. Sometimes the sea mists come riding over the downs, blotting out everything on their way, and settling in a damp dew. These are the days when elms and house and pergola stand out in silhouette. On the further side of the row of elms is a quite secluded nut walk that leads down to a barn, and on beyond is the fruit garden, diamond-shaped and enclosed with espaliers. In the centre is a dipping well, designed with as much care and precision as any part of the house. This little pool with the steps leading into the water is a charming retreat, for the apple trees gather round and recall the symbols and associations of the East, where the fruit trees were ceremoniously married to the well and life given to the garden.

These further parts of the garden seem to disappear imperceptibly away into orchards and trees, gradually escaping from the lines of the plan. The plan considered as pattern is curious. Though the house is symmetrical with

Little Thakeham: Viewpoint F on plan

Little Thakeham: Viewpoint G on plan

Little Thakeham, Sussex. Dipping well: Viewpoint H on plan

a strong central axis extending before it, the garden lies almost entirely to the south-east. There is an apparent want of balance about an axis that strongly calls for balance. In reality the orchards make up the balance and form a wide space introducing the view, which is thus drawn in as an integral part of the scheme. The excitements running round the house are held together by slender paths, and the whole area, including the house, is brought into relation with the bold simple terraces by the double hedge line that encloses them. Another small square garden, according to early plans, was intended to adjoin the lily pond, and this would have emphasized the unity of the group with the house. This medley is one part, the terrace is a second, and the lawn a third part of the main scheme that is to a certain extent linked together by the central walk. The weakest part of the scheme as it stands today is the stepped path that leads across the second terrace to the entrance to the pergola. Originally a more formal and interesting design was intended, but never carried out, to connect the lower to the upper garden. The elms are a perpetual foil to the long lines of the garden, and because the finest group is on the axis of the main lawn, and two more frame the way to the stables, they are as much a part of the scheme as the pergola itself.

Little Thakeham is one of the houses that followed the uncertain footsteps of Philip Webb or Norman Shaw. While those architects were heralding the return to the English tradition of Tudor or Elizabethan times, it was Sir Edwin Lutyens who first proceeded not merely to interpret the spirit of those times, but to carry on at the point where tradition was swamped by foreign influence. Probably the house might be criticised as being too traditional in form to be rational architecture of the day. The little devices that everywhere abound to hasten on surface effects usually given by time have become after twenty-five years of weathering rather superfluous. The design of the garden seems very much in advance of the house; it would be interesting to know how far Francis Bacon would have approved of these free ideas. Here is a technique in planning that is adjustable to every circumstance and situation, and the versatility that gives so much separate interest to a Lutyens garden. Little Thakeham is one of the least dramatic and its originality is not prominent. It settles into its surroundings as though it had been there always. Mundane fields and hedges were not a part of the English Landscape School, but circumstances now began to intermingle people again with the life that went on immediately around them. The lines of the garden at Little Thakeham were largely dictated by the very hedges that a few generations before were despised.

The climate in England is today presumably the same as it has ever been, but its influence on the immediate relation of house and garden varies considerably. In this house the interior is almost entirely cut off from the outside by the smallness of the windows. The treatment of the main hall, however, has an external quality, recalling the stonework immediately round the house. With changing circumstances of life, including modern heating, and communications that make the country accessible, the summer begins to be more important than the winter. In America, where the climate is certainly more inviting, the loose and open planning of airy spaces has the effect of almost drawing the garden through the house. The distribution of wealth is steadily making for the development of the smaller house, where requirements take precedence over studied effect, and so by the asymmetrical grouping that is always the logical expression of requirements, continues the work of drawing together house and nature. Against this is the gradual alteration of the whole countryside by the very quantity of these houses, only a few of which have any genuine consideration for their surroundings. Materials often can be brought more cheaply from longer distances than it is possible to acquire locally, and this means a standardisation that ignores the ground on which they rest. The speeding up of modern life, and a consequent decline in thought that is the natural outcome of hurry, tend towards buildings of a temporary rather than permanent character. Even now it is rare to see a garden planted for ten or twenty years hence, when it would not have been unusual in the past to plant only for posterity. Interest in our own garden lies in the immediate future, and soon there may be nothing of our own that will be worth passing on.

III

THE NATIONAL GARDEN

Though the great individual garden is passing, there rises the vaster problem of what may be called the national garden. In the country there are roads and village greens, views and spaces, and in a wider sense the care of the country itself. In cities there are parks, squares, boulevards, anywhere nature has been admitted purely for pleasure and refreshment. Such places in towns are not only for health; they are the sympathetic touch so vital to a community. To those especially who are unable often to reach the country, the crudest park or garden becomes beautiful by contrast, and the constant presence of beauty cannot fail to be ennobling. History shows how many towns have so benefited by being a part of the lay-out round an estate. The whole city of Carlsruhe in Germany emanates from the palace and its gardens; Richelieu, a town in France entirely built by the great statesman of Louis XIII, was itself dependent in design upon the garden of the château; the up-to-date suburban town of Versailles still contains the spirit of the Grand Monarch and his park. In the life of these places nature is only a dim, powerful background; the effect is more real if it has been brought into the streets themselves Because a town is the very heart of civilisation, nature is even more ordered than in a garden. The French have appreciated this, and with their grasp of ideas on a huge scale began a tradition under the monarchy that is being carried on today more grandly than in any country in Europe. The Boulevards and Champs Elysées carry into the heart of Paris the freshness of the country. The town of Nancy boasts one of the most charming municipal centres in the world, the whole character given to a rich architecture by a centre way of firmly clipped trees, under which pedestrians may walk or rest. At Nîmes, in the south of France, there are public gardens laid out on the ancient Roman baths, that must be among the most sumptuous and pleasant of any existing. Sometimes a city rampart has been altered from a place of war to one of peace. At Lucca, in Italy, the encircling walls are as grim and unyielding as ever; but the soldiers who manned the walls have been replaced by rows of trees that stand out stark against the evening sky. In a smaller way the public fountains in a city cheer by the sparkle and utter abandon of water. Rome in the seventeenth century is supposed to have had some hundreds of public fountains, fed by water brought at vast expense across the Campagna from the neighbouring hills. London has few of these integral delights, but it has the squares; as a part of the daily life they must be preserved for ever, for people need them as surely as they need the churches.

It is almost safe to say that no civic work of any magnitude can be undertaken without some immediate sacrifice on the part of the community concerned. There must be some noble instigation behind the enterprise, and that this is possible even in this materialistic world is told in the story that lies behind the gigantic lay-out of Chicago. In England the garden city movement is in each case the undertaking of a few individuals,

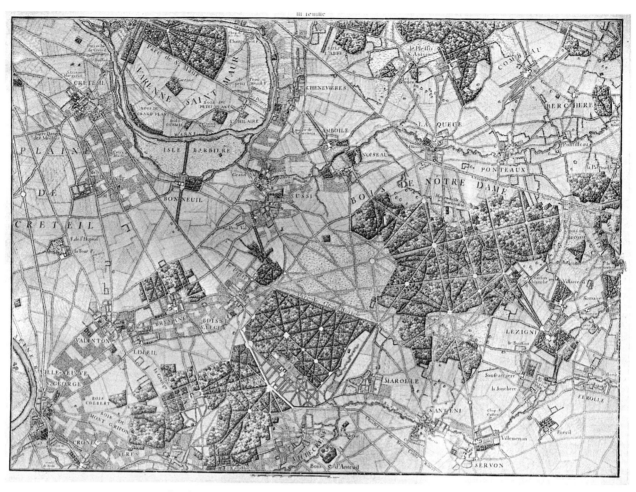

Artificiality of country round Paris. From a survey by Delagrive, 1740

but in reality it is the conception of a community where everyone has an equal share in the life around. At Hampstead Garden Suburb the spacious municipal centre between the two churches is reflected in those communal gardens that welcome every passer-by. Of her parks London is justly proud, and it is delightful to escape into them from eternal building. But they are not an integral part of London, not mixed up inextricably with the life as they try to be in Paris, bringing nature to the feet of the passer-by; rather the passer-by toils off to see the piece of nature so artfully trapped in his midst. However refreshing they may be, there is rarely anything great in these parks that would inspire as well as refresh the man in the street, and raise him unknown to himself from otherwise somewhat sordid surroundings. An exception is Kensington Gardens, for the trees and spaces are in stately unity with the outside world, as though the streets have shed the necessities of their existence, and existed only for the pleasure. How can the humblest remain unaffected when these tall, silent works of nature line his way? Similarly flowers can be intimately seen in the enclosed flower garden by the palace, where elsewhere their sweetness is lost in open beds whose chief merit is their lavishness and superb horticulture. Squares are different in character, and among the plane trees of Bedford Square and Gray's Inn, where the firm background of buildings is ever present, the charm lies in the pattern of slender forms and colour. It is one of the ironies of modern civilisation in England that these places, and similar places in

Public Gardens at Nîmes

Central Square, Hampstead Garden Suburb

the parks themselves, are hemmed in by railings. Iron railings are not necessarily ugly, but their very existence is against the suggestion of freedom. It is perhaps in the northern countries of Europe, particularly in Sweden, that the realisation of beautiful things in the everyday life of the people is most coming about, and it is true that the average standard of living is equivalently higher. Stockholm is called the Venice of the north,

Kensington Gardens, London

Gray's Inn, London

Public fountain at Zurich, Switzerland

and the town hall is the symbol of a national effort where many artists have worked, either in or on the building itself, or for the superb little public garden that stretches along the water front. In Central Europe, Zurich, the commercial capital of Switzerland, has developed an interest in public works that is almost as remarkable. While nature is being introduced into the towns, there is the meeting between town and country, and in a broader way the same problem arises as between house and country. There is the front to a seaside town. The sea sweeps from horizon to horizon, and in sympathy the front stretches more or less unbroken; gardens and flowers in such a position are not only lost, they are irritating. At Littlehampton, in Sussex, the houses have been set back a hundred yards or so, and the space in between was once an almost unbroken expanse of turf, echoing the sea beyond. Inland, towns are gradually eating up the countryside, sending out great feelers along the main roads, emanating not from the spirit that conceived a civic centre, but from that of commercialism. The old approach to Brighton, laid out by the Prince Regent, is one of the few in England worthy of the name. In the country itself, the villages are expanding indefinitely. In the Middle Ages they were the outcome of requirements; they grew up haphazardly, but the significance of the church led to its being the centre round which clustered the houses, making a natural composition. The materials from which they were built were acquired locally, and the effect today, after time has matured them, is that such places in their irregularity do indeed grow out of the country. When civic law began to take precedence over that of the church, the centre of interest moved to the actual life of the village, roads, markets, and above all the municipal centre. This meant the full significance of the Renaissance, the dignity of man asserting itself. From that moment the suppression of country has continued unmistakably throughout the centuries. This is not a sign of deterioration, for the finest works of man are in advance of the average state of nature – it is only at times that nature rises to that sublime perfection men cannot hope to attain. A certain artificiality was sometimes lent to the whole countryside by roads, the importance of which in the Renaissance was perhaps even greater than now.* The country round Paris is partially beautiful and partially dull, and it may have been this that led the French monarchy and nobility to connect their seats with great avenues that stretch across the countryside, changing its whole aspect. Today it is necessary in a far greater degree to co-ordinate vast areas, and though it is

'A network of roads, like veins, was strung over the land, interlacing, branching, dwindling to nothing...all the blood of the land flowed through these veins. The bumpy roads, gaping with dusty cracks in the sun, heavy with mud in the rain, were the moving life of the land, its breath and pulse.' From a description of Germany in the Renaissance in Jew Süss. *by Lion Feuchtwanger*

179

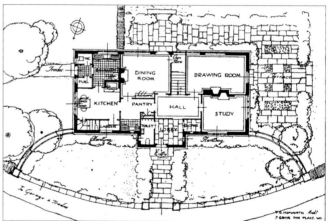

House in Devonshire. (By P. D. Hepworth, F.R.I.B.A.)

inevitable that the whole character of the countryside will soon be altered, it should be so altered to welcome rather than repel the stranger. There is real need for a combined effort, not to attempt to preserve the country as it is now, but to preserve the spirit of it in the form it is likely to take: skyline, groups of trees, water; hedgerows, fields, spaces that are waiting to be filled; moors and downs over which it is unreasonable to extend; colour; and above all a web of roads picking the logical way to their destinations. The great arterial roads with their attendant petrol stations, garages, and perpetual roar, give a basis of artificiality more dominant than at any previous period. These are the keynotes, and the subdivisions follow: roads spreading and linking together villages, and a countryside of scattered houses dependent on the roads and through these again on the countryside. In time roads may lose their significance, for science is a factor in modern life, a necessity that breaks down long accustomed barriers. It frees the world from the millstones to which it is used, and for a moment man stands amazed, lost in consternation. But tradition clings, and the complex persons who people God's earth remain the same; these things are not easily standardised.

BIBLIOGRAPHY

Atkinson, R., and Hope Bagenal: *Theory and Elements of Architecture.*
Blomfield, Reginald, M.A., F.S.A.: *The Formal Garden in England.*
Burckhardt, J.: *The Renaissance in Italy.*
Chambers, William: *A Disssertation on Oriental Gardening.*
Country Life Publications, including works by Gertrude Jekyll, H. Avery
    Tipping and Lawrence Weaver.
Fletcher, Banister, *A History of Architecture.*
Fouquier, M. and A. Duchene: *Des Divers Styles de Jardins.*
Gotch, J. Alfred: *The English Home.*
Gromort, Georges: *Italian Renaissance Architecture.*
Hegemann and Peets: *Civic Art.*
Von Humboldt, F.H.A.: *Cosmos.*
Repton, Humphrey: *Landscape Gardening.*
Sitwell, G.R.: *An Essay on the Making of Gardens.*
Stuart, C.M. Villiers: *Gardens of the Great Mughals.*
Triggs, F. Inigo: Publications on gardens.
Ward, W.H.: *French Renaissance Architecture.*
Wharton, Edith: *Italian Villas and their Gardens.*
Wijdeveld, H. Th.: *Life-work of Frank Lloyd Wright.*

GARDENS OF EUROPE

G.A. JELLICOE F.R.I.B.A.

First published 1937 by Blackie & Son Limited

To
My Mother

CONTENTS: GARDENS OF EUROPE

PREFACE

This book is based on three public lectures given at the Royal Institute of British Architects in 1936. It is intended mainly as a leisurely summary of *Italian Gardens of the Renaissance, Gardens & Design, Baroque Gardens of Austria, Garden Ornament and Decoration* and of articles such as *The Rhine Gardens* which have appeared from time to time in the architectural press. The first two books were written in collaboration with J.C. Shepherd, and from these most of the reproductions have been made.

G.A. Jellicoe
London 1937

1994 FOREWORD

Gardens of Europe is not an analytical and creative study like *Gardens & Design*, written a decade earlier. Rather it is one of those gentle ruminations that are an essential enrichment of the creative subconscious so clearly expressed by the sculptor Philip King in the introduction to Vol. IV.

It was while lying flat on my back on the floor of the basement of my office in John Street (later destroyed in the blitz) that I effortlessly dictated *Gardens of Europe* in two, maybe three, days. It came about because the publishers Blackie asked me to write such a travelogue with an advance of twenty pounds – an offer my purse of the time could not refuse.

While the turmoil of an architectural practice was continuing overhead, I returned in memory to browse over some fifteen years of historic landscape impressions. How agreeable were those two or three days soaked in the past, and how tempting to escape for ever from the haphazards of practice and become an art historian without material worries. Happily this was not to be, but it was twenty years before I began to write again with the theoretical *Studies in Landscape Design* (Vol. III) and forty years before I turned as a whole upon one's own work in the *Guelph Lectures* (Vol. IV).

Geoffrey Jellicoe
Highpoint 1995

ENGLAND AND SCOTLAND

At the outset, let me say that this travel through a hundred gardens to Rome follows a course that is purely imaginary. The gardens were visited over a period of twelve years, and the original routes are crossed and tangled. There appears, however, no reason why the general way of this book should not be followed.

I think it was the making of my own garden at All Cannings in Wiltshire that gave me the idea of going forth to see what other people had made of other gardens. Going forth, I mean, in recollection. When you have worked in a garden yourself, and realized the intense delight of flowers growing where there were none before, it seems a far distance to the great gardens of the Continent; but indeed we shall find that they, in their landscape, are as enjoyable as any of our own. So let us start without preamble.

Coming over the Plains to Salisbury, the traveller cannot help being inspired, like Constable, with what is perhaps the fairest cathedral landscape in England. The spire contrasts with the surrounding undulations, and is sufficiently large to rise above the groups of buildings of the surrounding city. This is the only cathedral in England, set in a spacious close, that was built at one period. Across the Green, and almost opposite the West Front, there is an unassuming house, behind which lies the most enchanting garden imaginable; a broad grass walk, with wide herbaceous borders on either side, leads in a straight line to the river. Turn about, and you see how beautifully composed is the long walk with the cathedral spire.

It is in some ways curious that such a simple garden should be so unforgettable, but this is the magic of garden design; and henceforth it will be a purpose, almost our first purpose, to find out and understand the reason of its power.

Dorset has always struck me as a county that has been overlooked, in comparison with its popular next-door neighbours, Devon and Cornwall. It is a county peculiarly rich in stone manor-houses, in a setting of pastureland and accompanying farms. Here the landscape of England is seen at its warmest, for in few places can the luxurious shapes of round-headed oaks, elms, beeches and other traditional trees be so appreciated in their relation to the rise and fall of the ground. It is no wonder that this sensuous relationship so inspired the poets and artists of the eighteenth century that they produced a new theme in garden design. The English School of Landscape Gardening grew out of a landscape that was first planted not for pleasure but for a practical purpose.

Very remote from any station, and set in a beautiful undulating valley, with the hills not too close, and a surrounding of trees, meadows and water, lies Bingham's Melcombe. This garden contains so many principles of design that we may well pause for a while and see how it came to be planned, and how the governing principles of over three hundred years ago apply to a garden laid out today. I always imagine that Bingham's Melcombe is to garden design in this country what Stonehenge is to architecture; in a sense it is the beginning of Planning.

You approach the house through a very ancient avenue, and enter under a gatehouse supposed to be haunted. The group of buildings round the

Cranbourne Manor. One of the great houses of Dorset

internal court is older than the garden, and there is no doubt that it was in Elizabethan times that the house was brought up-to-date. At that time the greater part of the garden was laid out. From the court, which is enriched by hydrangeas, you pass into what is now the living quarters, and almost before you are aware of it, have passed out again into the enclosed flower-garden. From this again you pass into the broader lines of the Elizabethan garden, upon a great length of bowling-green leading along the valley. On a high level, and parallel to the length extending from the house is a yew hedge, surely the finest in England.

   In exploring the garden, you are certain to visit this hedge, with its marvellous interlacing of branches. It is about a hundred yards long, nine-

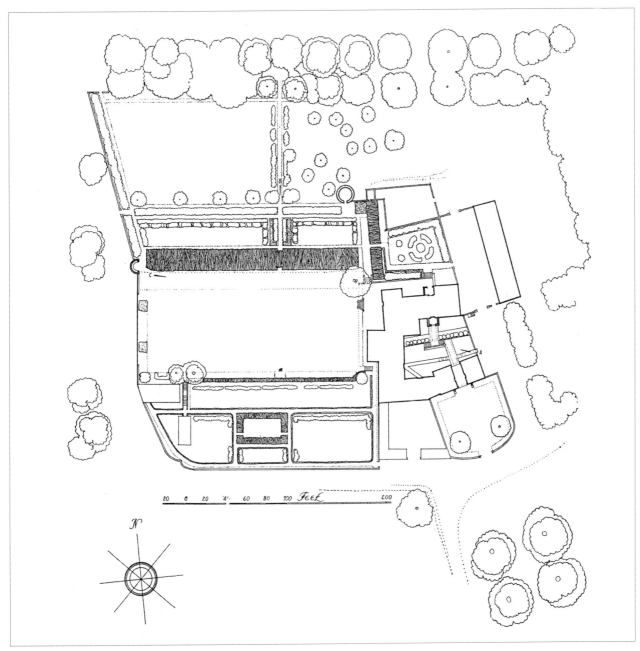

Plan of Bingham's Melcombe, Dorset

teen feet thick, and in perfect condition. Needless to say, the difficulties of clipping require a kind of running superstructure; but even this problem is slight in comparison with that of trespass. Already it has swallowed the adjoining terrace-path, and one wonders if even now its appetite is appeased. At the back of the yew hedge there is a delicious little orchard, and a path leads away into less formal woods. This new garden extends down the valley so that the bowling-green appears to be an extension from the house, and acts as a kind of broad platform. Although the garden is most simply laid out, there is no lack of variety. It inspires that curious feeling of dignity and repose which comes from a sense of appropriateness to purpose.

An analysis of the parts of the garden shows that there are two principal ideas only. One is the enclosed flower-garden, and the other is the great

Bingham's Melcombe, Dorset

open lawn. Nothing appears so simple and elementary as this primary use of materials. We know that flowers enjoy sun but require protection from wind; therefore it is logical that they should be placed in what amounts to a large open room. On the other hand, turf prefers open spaces, and as an expanse it is certainly easier to keep tidy than if it is cut up into a number of small beds. Thus we have the first principle of garden design; that materials should be placed in the position that is most suitable to themselves.

But we have to explore further into the secrets of Bingham's Melcombe, because the garden that is good horticulturally is not necessarily satisfactory to ourselves. At once we find a secret of garden design which was common knowledge in the days of the thoughtful designers of the past, but which has been mislaid during the course of years. In the flower-garden, we have the feeling that we are in a kind of additional room of the house, of which the sky is the ceiling. Thus we are drawn into the garden and conversely the scents of the flowers are distributed back into the house. It is a preparation for the wide open lawn, whose sense of spaciousness would otherwise be too far removed from the close interior for the human mind to appreciate. Nor is this the only secret that can be found by consideration of this garden, and when we have travelled farther and arrived at a famous landscape design in Northern Italy, superficially so different to this English garden, we shall discover how the bowling-green of Bingham's Melcombe appears to summarize the green meadows of the surrounding valley in the same way as the terrace of the Villa Cuzzano summarizes the valley in which it is set.

Somerset is a county so thinly populated that if we remove the towns of Bath and Bristol, the population per acre is almost the least in England. This is caused by large tracts of the Mendips and Exmoor, which give the county a very natural and wild landscape. Montacute is in a more sophisticated part, and this famous house, which was recently handed over to the National

Montacute, Somerset

Trust, is not only a delightful piece of architecture, but shows the evolution of garden design from sources other than horticulture and pleasure. The house itself is as curious a hybrid as any Elizabethan building. In it we see the tradition of Gothic architecture still persevering, and the trappings of the new style imported from Italy. Compared with the pure architecture of the Renaissance, Montacute can only be described as mongrel. Yet so ably have the details been elaborated, and so simply has the building been composed, that one can forgive the impurity in the sense of charm.

The gardens have been replaced somewhat on the original lines, but the centre area leading from the house towards the broad avenue in the meadow is original. This court has on either side raised walks, and over the balustrade it is possible to look down upon gardens, and into the park beyond. This is a typical plan of this period, and if the grandest example is undoubtedly Hatfield, the most attractive is Montacute. The garden is an extension of the facade of the house, and there is no reason why the façade should not be prolonged indefinitely into the surrounding country. When we come to visit Canon's Ashby, in Northamptonshire, we shall see a more developed example of this idea.

Let us now explore still further into the past, and see if we can trace the origins of the raised walk and garden houses at the corners, which form such a traditional set-piece of the garden design of this period. In the Middle Ages nearly all dwellings were so built that they were protected from outside. The country was disordered, and the most important and influential dwelling (if it can be described as such) was the castle. There were at this stage no external gardens. Within the castle walls, as within the walls of monasteries and other institutions, would be a formal garden in which were planted either special vegetables, sweet-smelling herbs, or particularly attractive and intimate flowers. This garden was a kind of extra room of the house, and the pattern of the design was somewhat similar to a carpet laid on the floor. Owing to troublous times, the persons most likely to enjoy the pleasures of existence that are suggested by a garden would be the women of the house. At times they would not be allowed beyond the castle walls, and one can imagine how they walked the ramparts in order to enjoy the landscape and the sense of space given by the view. Moreover, as the natural outcome of the choice of position, this view must in nearly all cases have been extensive as well as beautiful.

The standard form of castle, which had variations in plan but not in principle, was a square or other shape with towers at the corners. One can imagine that as the importance of the castle became less and less, so the walls became lower and were gradually extended and began to show the dwelling that stood inside. By the time of Elizabeth, these had been so flattened that the ramparts were mere raised walks, the turrets at the corners had become garden-houses, and the battlements were balustrades. In a later garden in Warwickshire, we shall see how the softening hand of civilization has still further subdued the wall, and introduced on the external side a row of built-in beehives. Thus can we trace the remarkable influence of tradition on garden design, and see how it may take a century to dispose of a feature that in the past formed part of everyday needs, and later had no function whatsoever.

Leaving behind us the spires of Montacute, our way leads again across Wiltshire, for by a long route we are to approach the handsome and once fashionable city of Bath. Adjoining Warminster, and not far from Westbury, lies Longleat, which can surely be described as one of the princely houses of England. Here is a perfect landscape of Elizabethan building set in a picture designed by the English School of Landscape Gardening. The house itself, with its seemingly endless pinnacles and turrets, is placed like a jewel in a setting of undulating park, of great groups of beech-trees that emphasize the lines and curves of the turf-covered ground. An avenue of elms, about a mile long, is the only formal link between house and outside world, which is finally approached through a massive and dignified entrance arch. So far is the whole idea behind this park removed from the early ramparts that inspired Montacute, that here again we may pause and consider how history has evolved a new art since the Elizabethan house was first built.

When the gardens of Montacute were laid out, and the still greater and more important formal gardens of Longleat, since destroyed, the influence of Italy was as yet not strongly felt in garden design. During the seventeenth century, however, it became fashionable to travel abroad, and distinguished amateurs like John Evelyn visited Italian gardens. These travellers returned with astonishing tales of the wonder of the Italian garden, of delights unheard of in England. But as so often happens the English traveller in Italy was unable in his short visits to understand and analyse the true principles of Italian garden design. He saw only the superficial beauty of their formality, taking note of the details of their architecture and losing the true secret that lies in their sense of planning and proportion. Yet to Evelyn and other famous travellers we owe a great debt of gratitude, for without them we might not have had until too late the law and order of Renaissance planning. But this formality that had come about by the end of the seventeenth century was not inherent in the English character. Its success lay in the fact that it was fashionable, and the fashionable world of that

Aerial view of Hatfield

period was anxious, as ever, to be up-to-date.

The progress of garden design after Montacute, therefore, is of a stricter formality and symmetry. Nowhere else is this indicated so strongly as in the Avenue. It became a fashion to have longer avenues, and more avenues. At Badminton, in Gloucestershire, avenues stretched out on all sides, and extended beyond the borders of the county. An arrangement was made with adjoining owners that these avenues could be continued across adjoining properties. Even more extraordinary than Badminton, perhaps, is the story of Boughton House, near Kettering. After the French wars of the early eighteenth century, the owner decided to relieve unemployment by tree planting, and endeavoured to obtain permission from Parliament to plant an avenue the whole seventy miles to London. This was not allowed, and the thwarted nobleman planted the same seventy miles of avenue on his own estate. Many of these avenues exist today, and lengths may be found here and there in the surrounding landscape.

There are few things in landscape design grander than an avenue, but even avenues can be overdone. Too much avenue is monotonous. It tends to drowse the senses. The eye is directed in a certain fixed way, and is not allowed to wander from one side to the other. The avenue is symbolical of the restraint that finally caused the romantic revival. In looking back upon this period of the early eighteenth century, it seems beyond belief that the culture of a nation could have been reversed in principle so rapidly and so successfully as to have influenced the whole of contemporary Europe.

I imagine that it was David Garrick who first crystallized the Romantic Movement. As usual it was the stage that foreshadowed the change in architecture. Previous to Garrick, the persons taking part in a production were known as 'players', and the audience was part of the spectacle. At no time was the audience under the illusion that the performance was anything but unreal, and if at any time they wished to join in, either with remarks or caustic comments, they certainly did so. There was no proscenium arch, and the audience more or less encircled an apron stage, on which the action took place. The words of a play were not spoken naturally, but rather by oratory. The choice of metre of the words was made with this end in view, in order that they might carry further in the open air.

This Garrick altered. He first saw the stage as a living picture, which the audience watched but did not take part in themselves. He introduced the curtain and the proscenium arch, and there appeared for the first time the Actor. It is said that so emotional could Garrick become, that the audience left night after night in tears.

This seems far removed from garden design, and especially from the park at Longleat, which caused us thus to wander. But in reality it is closely associated. In the formal garden, with straight comfortable paths, seats, and all the pleasures arranged beautifully for man's delight, man himself was part of the garden. In his rich costume he formed an additional decorative feature, and just as auditorium and stage in the theatre were one and the same, so were house and garden. With the coming of the English School of Landscape Gardening, the house remained the auditorium, but the surrounding landscape was considered not as being inspired by the work of man but by that of nature. It was a picture of ideal nature. The common meadows, undulations and groups of trees that form the English landscape were idealized into what is now known as the English park. French painters were the first of the artists to realize this emotional beauty of landscape, and the paintings of such men as Watteau came to be considered for their landscape groupings.

The story of the change from formal to the landscape is one of the most interesting and astonishing in all the history of garden design. Alexander Pope was right to satirize the peculiarities of existing fashion. He it was who poured such ridicule as to say of an imaginary sale of clipped hedges . . . 'A quickset hog shot up into a porcupine, by its being forgot a week in rainy weather.' Horace Walpole built Strawberry Hill, in which he epitomized the idea of romance which lay behind the whole movement. Not only was a new view taken of landscape, but the buildings of the past, castles, monasteries, ruins, anything with a glamour of history, were made things of absorbing interest. Life must be lived in ideal surroundings, and great classic buildings came to be set in parks from which all connexion with the outside world must be excluded. There must be no boundaries, and thus was invented the sunk ditch, or 'ha-ha'. Why 'ha-ha' no one has been able to say, except that it clearly came as a surprise. There were even to be no approach drives to the house, but the experiment of growing moss on gravel was soon abandoned. But while the drive approach could not be easily hidden, that to the servants' quarters did not present such a difficult problem. In many instances, such as at Claremont, near Esher, there would be a tunnel of such a length that the mouth would be far enough from the house not to be seen from it.

There must be no straight lines in this ideal landscape, for straight lines are made by man and are not natural. Thereby came about the undulating drive; which had, however, an apparent reason for its curves, either to follow the natural contours of the ground or to avoid obstacles. If an obstacle were not there to give a reason for the curve, it was made. In order to enliven the landscape with romance, ruins were sometimes added, and in one case even a church whose steeple was only half a steeple, and the church itself a gardener's cottage.

These ideas sound idle when you walk through Longleat Park and see how beautifully the water of the lake reflects the curving shapes of hills, and gives a lusciousness to the picture. It was not, however, Capability Brown who was really responsible for the great works of this period, so much as his follower, Humphrey Repton. While Brown was trained as a gardener only (acquiring his nickname through his astonishing facility for the acquisition of work and the alteration of noblemen's existing gardens), Repton was a serious student of architecture as well as landscape. He it was who appreciated that a house is primarily to be lived in, and if set in a picturesque landscape must have some connexion between itself and the curving lines of nature. He reintroduced the terrace, and indeed was able to analyse the true meaning of the straight line as opposed to the curving line. One likes to think of the indefatigable Repton producing his series of reports – the little Red Books – while in a coach bumping from place to place.

Of all the contributions to landscape design made by Humphrey Repton, none is so significant as his desire to let the imagination roam. In contrast to the avenue that leads the eye in one direction, Repton arranged the landscape so that it appeared to have no finish. There is a wholeness about an English park of this period; it gives a complete picture of house, landscape and sky. Where the eye roams over a hill, and cannot see the other side, the mind tends to fill in imaginings of its own. As we take one last look at Longleat, we can follow our imagination roaming among groups of trees, and up and over the undulations upon which they stand.

While this park is a perfect example of a complete landscape, Prior Park, overlooking Bath is perhaps the unique example of the landscape arranged as a picture, to be seen from one point of view only. The great house stands at the head of a valley which leads down to Bath, a mile or two away. On either side, round groups of trees stand like stage scenery, and in the middle distance at the centre of the picture is a Palladian bridge. This bridge also has no function whatever, and in terms of cost at the present day would represent more than one small house.

How pleasurable it is in this age of utility to find something doing nothing! This architecture can express no serious purpose, because it has nothing but a dream to express.

So well is this view composed within its frame that it must certainly have been inspired by the painters. Here too we appreciate another great factor of this period of landscape design. The human being in modern dress, and indeed even in contemporary dress, is out of place, for this picture has been conceived as something similar to the legends of the past and is timeless. Just as a formal garden requires costumed people to complete its design, so

Prior Park, Bath

the illusion of the landscape park is broken by their presence. This curious and interesting theme has been followed throughout history, and there is a record of a party in this sensitive age to which gentlemen in bearskins only were invited.

It is no wonder that such a fine site was available for Prior Park, for all round the city are green hills covered with grey buildings and walls. When Bath was fashionable, and before the view over the city was impaired by nineteenth-century additions, these views must have been lovely beyond words.

Continuing our journey north, we go up and down some brisk hills for a few miles, and after some difficulty run to earth a very early garden called St. Catherine's Court. This little group of buildings and church is placed on the side of a hill, within a fairly close valley, and the garden runs upwards in a series of steep terraces. The garden is Elizabethan, and is one of the few in this country in which the terraces look down upon the house.

St. Catherine's Court is attractive in its landscape setting, but has not the peculiar fascination that seems always to embrace Owlpen Manor. This lies in the Cotswolds, a few miles further north, and suggests the first garden in England that was laid out beyond the walls of a castle. Historically this is probably incorrect, although parts of the garden are certainly Tudor with early Stuart additions. But no one can be in Owlpen two or three hours without the feeling of mystery and oppression that is characteristic of the Middle Ages. The valley in which it lies is steeper and closer and even more remote than that around St. Catherine's Court. The little group of buildings consists of the Manor itself, some adjoining farm buildings, and immediately above the house a small church.

The garden is very simply laid out on the earliest principle, that of extension of the façades of the house on either side. Owing to the hillside, this gives a series of steep terraces. In the angle between the two extensions of the façades is now a mighty parlour, a kind of square room with walls of ancient yew, within which you can imagine all sorts and kinds of witchcraft. Elsewhere there are other yews standing individually, but some of these,

Owlpen Manor, Gloucestershire

together with the whole of the woods that crowned the slopes at the back, have recently been cut down. You cannot ruminate easily in Owlpen garden, owing to the general sense of oppression; but let us cross the valley and pause a moment to think of the meaning of this early garden.

From this vantage point, you will realize how the group is entirely enfolded by the hills. It is almost as though the design has grown from the hillside, and is similar to the idea of growth in Gothic architecture. The intense steepness of the site makes for a certain discomfort in such things as steps; and it is interesting to imagine how gardens gradually came to be built on less awkward sites, and how the choice of gentler, undulating ground introduced a sense of well-being. Between Owlpen and Hampton Court is written the story of the growth of man's intense enjoyment of the present moment, the keynote of the Renaissance.

Curiously enough, it is not far from Owlpen that we find the best example in this country of what might be described as a satisfied garden. If we were going by air, we should fly straight across the River Severn, seeing below us first the escarpments of the Cotswolds, with their groups of beech-trees and stone walls; then the checkboard plain, with the white river beyond; and far away in the distance the tower of Gloucester Cathedral. In front are the blue wooded hills of the Forest of Dean. Westbury Court lies on the farther side of the Severn in a local flat landscape reminiscent of Holland.

Westbury was laid out by a partisan of William and Mary, and although the house itself has been pulled down, sufficient remains of the garden to show all the characteristics of the Dutch influence. How often do we collect ideas from the Continent, absorb them, and form an art that is still essentially English. First there is the French influence in Gothic architecture, slightly affecting gardens. Then in late Tudor and Stuart days, Italy is predominant. With the advent of William and Mary, Dutch architecture is studied and to this period belongs some of our best domestic work. The rise of Louis XIV and the French wars brought a French influence, and in certain large formal landscape designs like the Mall, we see the hand of the great French landscape architect Le Nôtre. The English School of Landscape Gardening certainly created an art of its own, and through this we have given to the Continent as much as we have received. So much so, in fact, that during the nineteenth century many fine formal gardens abroad were destroyed and their place taken by what is known as the 'Giardino Inglese'.

The great quality of Westbury is its sense of repose. This is given by long lines of canals, brick walls and clipped hedges. To contrast with this repose is the spire of the parish church, itself a very curious piece of church architecture, and it would seem that the garden was planned so that this spire should act as a foil. There are two charming little garden-houses, built of the same mellow brick as the walls. One of these terminates a canal, and the other is an example of what is found very often in Holland itself. The Englishman has a peculiarity in common with the Dutchman: he is intensely interested in what his neighbour is doing, but does not like his neighbour to know what he himself is doing. These little garden-houses are so built on canals or roads in Holland, that the owner can sit inside and watch the passing world, without being visible himself. But if at Westbury the garden-houses are symbolical of one point of view, the two clairvoyees in the wall by the road express another – the community sense. As you pass along a hot road, you have a refreshing glimpse of water, green turf and pleasant trees.

Passing north through Gloucestershire, we can follow the range of oolite hills that pass across England from Dorset to Yorkshire, now showing slight undulations, now rising to a thousand feet. They rise to their highest at Cleeve Cloud, near Cheltenham, and the area known as the Cotswold reaches its greatest depth between Bibury and Broadway. Possibly the villages and towns of the Cotswolds are in the aggregate the most famous in England. This is due to the contrast of the bleak hills with the homely buildings nestling in the valleys; and also because their architecture mostly dates from a period of great prosperity in the wool trade, coinciding with one of the best periods of architectural design. These hills and vales, which certainly are most majestic along the whole length of their west escarpment, are by no means original landscapes. It was only in the eighteenth century that the stone walls that are now such a characteristic feature were built, and the great clumps of beech-trees planted. Cirencester is perhaps the most important town, and it is worth noting that the beech-trees in the park are supposed to be self-seeded from the original trees that covered the Cotswolds in prehistoric times. The park is romantically planned in relation to the town, and the great semicircular hedge in front of the house is a tribute to the hedge-clipper.

The Cotswolds contain in their midst a number of delightful gardens, for the grey stone is an admirable building material. The possibility of conveying cheap material long distances by modern transport has altered local characteristics not only here, but throughout England. We have only to walk from the edge of the Cotswolds to the Vale of Evesham to see as great a variety as is possible in a small area. Thus it was logical to build

Westbury-on-Severn, Gloucestershire

houses and gardens of stone if these were placed either in the Cotswolds, or where stone could be brought from the quarries by gravity. The moment we leave the slopes, we find half-timber in use, and thereafter brick.

A geological map of England shows an immense variety of subsoil material which can be called upon for building. The great oolite range alone claims a variety of stone that changes from the grey of the Cotswolds to the yellow of Northamptonshire. In other parts different clays have produced different bricks. In the east country, where roads were bad and even local transport difficult, we find the use of material limited to the lightest possible, such as half-timber and plaster, or weather-boarding. Each area of England, moreover, has its own traditions and methods of building, which in turn add to the variety. To travel across England from one county to another at the time when these historical gardens were made, must have been like travelling from one country to another today.

There are many gardens which we should glance at before leaving the Cotswolds, though there is none that we can justly describe as *the* garden of the Cotswolds. Somewhat apart and surrounded by the Vale of Evesham, lies Overbury Court, on the south slopes of Bredon Hill. With its wealth of water, and surroundings of meadows, parish church and village, it is as delightful a place as any from which to look across the Vale to Gloucester. The village of Broadway contains some good gardens behind its fronts, and is indeed almost a garden in itself. The combination of village street and the curve of beech-crowned hills is one of the finest landscape pictures existing, the inspiration of which dates again from the period of the English School of Landscape Gardening.

We cannot leave this part of the world without making a pilgrimage to Oxford, and on the way we pass two or three places at which we must glance.

Dytchley. The north-west terrace

Chastleton Manor was built in the early seventeenth century, and is an interesting example of the architecture of that time. It was built for a wool magnate, who appears to have followed the course adopted by magnates of today, by building in the style of a previous century. It is a massive building, but in design it cannot be compared either with the buildings it set out to copy, or its own contemporaries. Its setting is particularly attractive, while to one side lies a topiary garden that is almost unbelievable, so varied is the manner of clipping.

Returning to the Worcestershire and Oxford road, we soon come to Enstone, and are within range of three great houses built almost at the same time. The first is Heythrop, designed by Vanbrugh; the second is Dytchley, built by James Gibbs; and the third and most important, is Blenheim Palace, built by Vanbrugh. It appears that the Earls of Lichfield, having decided to pull down their existing house at Dytchley, came to the conclusion that three houses by Vanbrugh in a small district would weigh too heavily upon the earth, so Dytchley was given to Gibbs and came to be accepted as his domestic masterpiece. House and park are an English scene of grey stone and gracious beeches.

The gardens are modern, but they give food for thought as to how the grand manner in garden design can be continued in this country, and how modern methods and inventions since the eighteenth century have given rise to variations in design. The gardens at Dytchley are based on a print left by Gibbs, on which were indicated three or four lines suggesting the lay-out. Possibly the most noticeable variation from an eighteenth-century design

Aerial view of Blenheim Palace and grounds

would be the two spacious stone terraces, west and north. These suggest that entertaining is possible at much closer intervals than in the old days. It is now easy for a Londoner to travel sixty or seventy miles and return the same night; whereas in the eighteenth century, visitors would be confined to those living within a comparatively small radius.

Another feature at Dytchley which is a variation upon the past is the use of water. Electric power has made possible fountains on a scale previously unconsidered in this country. Nor was water urgently required as in France or Italy, for our climate is moist. In the choice of site the consideration of where a reservoir could be made at sufficient height to give power to fountain display was not considered paramount. Today it is possible to press a button in the house and set machinery under way, which will send the jets of thirty or forty fountains as many feet into the air, for as long or as short a time as you wish.

Five miles farther on the road to Oxford is the charming little township of Woodstock, and I imagine that to walk up the main street, and burst suddenly upon the view of Blenheim as seen beyond the great entrance arch, is to experience the grandest sensation that it is possible to feel from any designed landscape. It is in a sense almost a pity to continue to walk round the estate, so magnificent and breath-taking is this first sight. The building of Blenheim is, of course, a classic. How Vanbrugh did in fact grapple with Sarah, Duchess of Marlborough, and produce the mightiest pile of stone in England (when all that Her Grace required was a modest country house), is a mystery that no biographies and no productions on the stage have been able quite to clarify. Whether you like Blenheim, or think it is a nightmare of stone and mortar, you must admit that it is a mighty conception, mightily carried out. There are few who do not at least admire the great bridge across the lake.

We have called the sheet of water at Blenheim a lake, but this would be an insult to the co-designer of the park, our energetic friend, Capability Brown. Certainly the mingling of the gigantic formal pattern design by Vanbrugh with the free natural lines of Brown are remarkable. The trees of Vanbrugh's great avenue have only recently been re-planted, but it is said that they are planted in the formation of the army at the Battle of Blenheim. As for Capability Brown, he so altered and dammed the small existing stream as to give an effect of continuity to the lake. As he stood on the terrace before the house, he is said to have cried out: 'Thames, Thames, wilt thou ever forgive me?' for having produced a river that outrivalled anything in this country. Ground modelling is perfectly shown at Blenheim, and it is all the more remarkable when we realize how many years ahead the designer must have visualized his design of green trees come to fruition.

There is little pomp and splendour in English garden design that can compete with the great French and Italian gardens, and as we leave Woodstock on the road to Oxford, we can at least be satisfied that there is one place in England that can hold its own in point of grandeur with any yet to come.

The towers and spires of Oxford, seen across a foreground of meadows, are unforgettable. It gives a glimpse of how many another city must have appeared in the Middle Ages, when buildings were huddled together within surrounding walls, and outside lay the open country. It is one of the tragedies of our day that this fair city should be slowly surrounded by sporadic and bad development. How short-sighted has been the policy of preserving the interior and letting the fringes be spoiled! Soon it may not be possible even to imagine the beauty of such a city in an English landscape.

The High is unquestionably one of the great streets of the world, and it is a clue to the crowded splendour that lies on either side. These huddled groups of buildings, so beautiful in their architecture, have always seemed to me to epitomize the peculiarities of learning. The jostling of so many buildings, mostly without any relationship between one College and another, would be impossible in a community that had considered at any time a far-sighted policy in architecture. Yet it is this very jostling that makes Oxford so human a document.

Oxford was one of the earliest centres of gardening in this country. Old prints show how the early progress of garden design has developed from the Middle Ages until an open garden was possible. Undoubtedly the gardens of these Colleges were looked upon as extensions of the internal rooms into a series of compartments. At Bingham's Melcombe, a single enclosed flower-garden alone is attached to the house. In Oxford, the garden very often consisted of a series of rooms each containing a variety of plants. It was at this period that the idea of a Mound became of importance. The Mound gave the opportunity of observing from a secluded vantage-point

Canon's Ashby, Northamptonshire

what happened outside the court, and many a modern garden contains one of these features which have a sentimental background of history.

Surrounding Oxford are a number of delightful eighteenth-century houses and gardens, which it is not possible for us to visit. We must, however, take a glance at Pusey House, between Faringdon and Abingdon, for it is probably one of the most enchanting examples of domestic landscape of its period. The house is supposed to have been built by Wood of Bath, who had previously built Prior Park as a speculation to encourage the use of Bath stone in construction. Pusey has four curved walls leading out symmetrically from the main block, and is so poor in its architectural detail as to be positively decadent. In front of the house are great groups of beech-trees, with turf running away in between apparently without boundaries; and upon the turf is a cricket pitch.

On the farther side is a strip of water seeming, since its ends are concealed, to be a river similar to that at Blenheim. Beyond is a distant view of the Berkshire hills. There is no feature about Pusey that one can say is exceptional, or better than what we have already seen, but one can certainly say that there are few places in England where house, landscape and sky form a more complete composition.

Leaving behind Oxfordshire's attractive but rather undernourished agricultural landscape, we continue on the oolite range in order to visit Canon's Ashby in Northamptonshire. The grey stone of Oxfordshire has changed its colour to yellow, and the landscape has become richer. The group at Canon's Ashby is another example of those delightful compositions of manor house, outbuildings, and church, almost enveloped in trees, that are such a characteristic of this type of English domestic architecture. There are many people who are not sure whether the yellow Northamptonshire stone appeals to them, but I should be surprised if they could resist the stone of Canon's Ashby turning to golden-brown in the sun.

The house dates from an earlier period than the garden, but was rebuilt in the early seventeenth century, and the lay-out extended on either side of the two façades. The north façade has in front a simple forecourt, but the west façade is continued down a slope in a series of different sized terraces, containing grass, trees and flower-gardens; until finally the axis is carried away into an avenue. The simplicity of this idea is such that the architectural lines form a background which emphasizes all the trees that are planted upon it. One of the cross-paths centres upon the church tower. All this work was carried out at the time of the re-fronting of the house, but in the following century the landscapists became fashionably busy. Here, however, they confined their work to collaboration with the formal design, and laid out as a picture the view seen from the angle formed by the two gardens projecting from their façades. Decision between architecture and nature has been so well marked that no designer intrudes upon another's ideas; it is this definition that gives to Canon's Ashby that extraordinary sense of peace, that time alone cannot ensure.

Our next objective is Compton Winyates in Warwickshire, the only garden which it is preferable for us not to enter. Indeed, if one were not interested in interior architecture, no greater excitement could be found than by sitting on one of the neighbouring slopes and contemplating this strange irregular pile, one of the most famous domestic buildings in this country. As with so many early buildings, one senses the relationship to the surrounding semicircle of hills. Modest gardens are laid out with rich topiary outside the moat, but you will know that for all their excellence they spoil the ideal of an early English landscape. Compton Winyates is like some strange natural object rising from the ground, and so closely associated is it with landscape that it needs none of those introductory lines that form part of more classic building. Here is the idea of haphazard growth, and although gardens are contained within the moat, it is alien to the true idea of history that they should extend outside.

If Compton Winyates is strange, it is not to be compared with Packwood House, not very far away in the same county. The first part of Packwood was laid out on Elizabethan lines, and here we see a small example of the raised terrace, with gardens at either side. Round the terrace and the house are four borders, as one would expect. It is only when we walk up the terrace, or through the garden gates, that we behold a fantasy in garden design that is unequalled in this country, or for that matter, anywhere.

In the seventeenth century, Packwood belonged to a cleric who was a fanatic in both religion and gardens. This combination produced the idea that he should plant the whole story of the Sermon on the Mount in yew. From the terrace you see a crowd of mighty yews, all clipped to different cone-shapes. Penetrating this assembly, you approach twelve more regular yews, which are the Apostles; and in the centre, mightier than the others, spiral in shape and raised on a mound, stands the Teacher. Of course the idea is enchanting, and so beautiful are the colours of the yew, and so reasonable the surrounding Warwickshire elms, that you feel that in spite of its peculiarity, it can be a garden as lovable as any. Besides, it is in the wall of a terrace facing the crowd that are built the little semicircles of brick containing beehives, and bees give a sense of reality.

Reviewing as a whole the distribution of gardens in England, there is no

Compton Wynyates, Warwickshire

Packwood House, Warwickshire

doubt that they are most plentiful in the west and south. The eastern counties are flat, and although they contain numerous fine houses, they do not seem to have produced the same number of distinguished gardens as elsewhere. The north of England, which we are now approaching, has clearly been less inviting for the building of country seats, and vegetation is appreciably less luxuriant than in the south. It is said that the north never recovered from being laid waste by William the Conqueror, and whether this is appreciable at the present day or not, it is certainly safe to say that it placed a drag on landscape garden development that was still felt in the eighteenth century.

In passing through Derbyshire, we must call at Melbourne Hall, for here are more formal yew walks than in any other garden; apart from the fame of its clipped hedges, it is also one of the few places whose garden sculpture and ornament can equal those on the Continent. The road by Derby to Matlock threads its way through rocky dales, and thence to a valley dominated by the princely house of Chatsworth. Before entering this valley, we should have a look at Haddon Hall, just adjoining, for Haddon is romantically situated and has perhaps the most beautiful of all English garden stairs.

Entering the valley of Chatsworth, which is long and narrow, and threaded by the river, we appreciate at once that here is another of those landscapes that have been 'organized' on a grand scale. The great house is placed on the lower slopes, about midway across the length. The whole of its park, within visible distance, has been arranged, and in contrast to such another park as Longleat, has introduced as part of its design not only the rich luscious hardwood trees, but conifers that tell of the bleak Derbyshire moors that approach the rim of the hills. The private gardens at Chatsworth are as princely as the house, and it was here that Sir Joseph Paxton was head gardener, building the great glasshouse that was the predecessor of his design for the Crystal Palace. But unquestionably consideration of the whole valley as a single unit is the greatest contribution to the history of garden design that is made by Chatsworth.

Our next objective is Bramham Park in Yorkshire, a lay-out that it is essential for anyone to visit who is interested in the development of formal parks. The house and forecourt are themselves superb examples of eighteenth century domestic architecture, but the lay-out is one of those vast compositions that were obviously inspired by the French. Again it is said that Le Nôtre prepared the design, and it is certainly more possible in this case, since there are so many characteristics found in France alone. There is a magnificent water garden, but finest of all at Bramham Park are surely the great avenues, which interlace and cut across the close-wooded park like a French forest. Yet if we compare one of these avenues with those of Versailles, we see that the great trees have grown up and arched overhead of their own accord, in a way that Le Nôtre would not have allowed. In these avenues we can see how the Englishman succumbs to the personality of trees, and how the idea of growth came to be part of Gothic cathedral architecture.

Were we more easily diverted from our course of gardens, we should visit some of the great houses of the north, like Castle Howard. We should

Bramham Park, Yorkshire

certainly visit the Lake District for its natural landscape, for here is an area
so strong in character that we neither expect nor desire to find a great
garden laid out by the hand of man. But we must push on to Scotland, for
we have many miles of Highland country to traverse.

Arbigland is a country house situated on the shores of the Solway Firth,
themselves notable for a climate that is almost tropical. Away across the
water looking south are seen the heights of the Lake District: Skiddaw,
Helvellyn, and the assembled throng of mountains with their accompanying
clouds. Beautiful as is the site of Arbigland itself, it is the walled flower-
garden that has drawn us from our direct route to the North. This is a
diagonal in the midst of trees that stretch down to the water's edge.
Guarding the exit to the east, and at the point of the diagonal facing south,
are twin circular houses that act as bastions against the south-west gales.
This enclosed sea-garden, so far north of the English Channel, must be
unique.

In the hills round Arbigland there is a hint of the Scottish Highlands, and
as our way leads north from Dumfries to Thornhill we feel the beginnings
of a scenery that is majestic. The approach to Drumlanrig Castle is itself
dramatic. The drive leads towards and over a mighty bridge, winds round
through a wild park and suddenly enters a broad avenue finished at the end
by the great building bristling with towers. The castle itself was built in the
early seventeenth century, but the tradition of ruggedness has been
continued. The architect seems to have toyed a little with Italian detail, but
has never shaken free of history. This makes the castle in its landscape one
of the most impressive of its kind. You must imagine the sun lighting up the

pink stone, and all around a tumbling, conifer-crowned landscape, penetrating at times as far as the building itself. The austerity of the mound upon which the castle stands, and the retaining wall in front, is magnificent. Like the princely Chatsworth this castle appears to organize the whole of the vast, wild landscape in which it is set.

The farther north we continue in Scotland the more immense becomes the scenery, and the less important we ourselves feel. The road we take winds its way through the purple clad mountains of the Grampians. Here and there stands out in contrast a white cottage or group of buildings. When at last we reach Braemar and the luscious valley that extends from here to Ballater and thence to the coast, we feel that we have reached a haven of comfortable houses, parks and gardens.

The care that Queen Victoria took in choosing the site for Balmoral has certainly been justified, and there is something peculiarly engaging in the granite spires and towers of this Royal Scottish seat. It is, indeed, a climax of all the residences of the valley, where gardens are luxurious and flowers flourish remarkably. I imagine the valley of the Dee to be the most complete picture we have of a nineteenth century continuous landscape.

We are now at the most northern point of our travels, and so far from our course that I think we should do well to quicken our return to the south. We will, therefore, take to the air and fly direct to that Mecca of all lovers of the English garden, Hampton Court. On our way we can pick out the turrets and enclosed gardens of Glamis. After crossing the sea for a while we join land and pass over the broad Cheviots, to be once more above English soil. As we fly south we see how the complicated pattern of the English fields becomes richer with trees. Durham Cathedral stands out rivalling the Austrian Melk in splendour of landscape. We pass towns, scattered hamlets, and great country houses. We see, in short, a panorama of landscape, for this route will cross the lines of geological strata and expose all the variations of the English scene.

It is fitting that Hampton Court should be our terminus in England, because it appears to summarize all that is meant by the English tradition of garden design. This palace means to the English monarchy what Versailles means to the French. When we compare the two, and observe the warm red brick and bristling chimneys of the one, and the white marble and stone of the other, we realize how strong has been the force of *domestic* as opposed to *monumental* architecture in this country. It is the echo of a constitution essentially democratic. When we cross to Paris, we shall see that the monarchy could attract to the capital the whole of the French nobility. Almost all the great gardens of the seventeenth and eighteenth centuries in France are to be found within an hour's journey of Paris. In England there was no such concentration, and we find the nobility building their houses on estates which by wise exploitation had in many cases produced their wealth. Thus the traditional English house has literally grown from the soil and from the landscape which it came to dominate. This adherence to the soil naturally produced a more domestic outlook, and even when Christopher Wren was commissioned to add a new east façade to Hampton

Drumlanrig Castle. The Terrace

Court, this retained its character of domesticity. The gardens are laid out on a series of ascending scales, starting with the tiny copy of a Tudor knot-garden, and followed quickly by what is known as the small Dutch garden. Thence one passes into the larger and beautifully planned garden of Christopher Wren, with the two raised terraces on either side; and so out into the broad semicircular garden laid out in the time of William and Mary. This largest garden, with its converging avenues, is based on the work of Le Nôtre, and there is no doubt of its beauty. Originally the centre of the semicircle was planted with box parterre in patterns, and it was Anne, homely soul, who removed the elaboration and planted the grass as it is today. All that remains of the original parterre is the umbrella yews, which

Hampton Court

were probably never intended to be more than three or four feet high.

Of course if you go to Hampton Court, you go to see the herbaceous border. And very distinguished it is, too, though you may feel that it is a little lost in the broad area of gravel that lies in front. How comparatively new in idea must be the herbaceous border! One imagines that the original little flower-garden at Bingham's Melcombe would be sufficient to show the variety of plants available at the time. As the world came to be combed for more and more specimens, so not only was more room required, but the plants themselves became larger. The herbaceous border has come to be almost an essential part of every English garden, but its origin does not go very far into the past, and it is another example of how the experiences of time introduce new requirements. Yet the principles of horticulture in the lay-out of the herbaceous border are the same as have always applied to flower-gardens. To see the long border at Hampton Court, with its background of red brick wall, is to feel that close association between planting and protection that is a lasting secret of the enjoyment of flowers.

So from Hampton Court we go south across the Weald of Sussex, which is as rich in small cottage gardens as it is in those of manor houses. We should explore some of the gardens of the South Downs. But as Hampton Court appears to have summarized the whole of English Gardens, we had better hasten across the long hills of the South Downs and for our next stage pass over the sea.

FRANCE, GERMANY, AUSTRIA

It may be that in the course of time international relations will remove national characteristics, and that to cross the Channel will show no great change in ways of living. While it has been possible to go through the varied landscape of England, and to pass from a small cottage-garden to the largest garden without any serious feeling of discomfort, it is not possible to do so from a great garden of England to one in France. There is something so fundamentally, racially different, that the transition is too abrupt. In England one feels that the trees, turf and flowers are the same for all gardens, and that these materials predominate over everything else.

Let us forget about England, therefore, and like the genii of old, cause ourselves to be materialized upon the central steps of Chantilly. Here is a strange, fantastic and magnificent world indeed.

The first impression of Chantilly is of a vast open space enriched by patterns of water, parterre, gravel paths, great flights of steps, and mighty avenues. Thereafter you see the palace and the group built later on the opposite side of the central axis. When the Grand Condé decided to lay out the garden in the sumptuous fashion of the time, he stipulated to Le Nôtre that the existing mediaeval palace must be retained. The palace as it stands today is a replica of the original, which was burned down during the last century. To Le Nôtre, the palace seemed too small and ineffective to become a central feature, and he therefore laid out the principal lines of

Chantilly

the garden not to lead upon the building but to run out into the country on either side. Where these lines passed the house he placed a noble flight of steps, which led to a forecourt containing in the centre a statue of the Prince himself. Thus it is that the whole of the great gardens at Chantilly are as it were suspended upon this statue, and epitomize at once the secret of French gardens of the age of Louis XIV. They stood for the glorification of man, and of France, and they ruled the gently undulating landscape upon which they were laid.

So immense was the output of garden design during the period of *le roi soleil* that the design of the French garden seems almost an accomplished fact without a background of history. The gardens of Italy and England may be traced in their development stage by stage. The same must apply to any form of art, and if it is less obvious in France, the growth of the principles of Le Nôtre's design can be traced to their original sources. If we examine the eighteenth century maps by the Abbé Delagrive, we find the whole of the contemporary landscape around Paris shown in beautiful detail. The first characteristic that strikes one is the criss-crossing of the hunting forests. Adjoining the Forest of St. Germain is the Château de Maisons, which was built and laid out by François Mansart prior to Le Nôtre. The park shows an intermediary stage of design, between purely utilitarian hunting avenues in the forests, and a fully developed design by Le Nôtre. In it we see how the sense of pattern underlying these forests has been realized as a decorative feature, and turned into a piece of embroidery.

If this is the source of Le Nôtre's main inspirations, another undoubtedly lies in the traditional love of water that followed the Kings of France. It was love of water that caused the buildings of the Châteaux upon the Loire, whose architecture flourishes like plants beside a river.

The third great element of French garden design is spectacle. These gardens are frankly designed for entertaining, and since the average size was intended to hold not less than two or three thousand people, each in a costume incredibly rich in comparison with those of today, it is not un-natural that their open expanses of gravel appeared empty between entertainments. It is safe to say that the French garden was intended to be and to appear emptier than is normally expected of a garden, in order that people should actually be required to complete the design.

The first great spectacle in a French garden was held at Vaux-le-Vicomte, south of Paris, on 17th August, 1661. The creator of this new wonder was the Finance Minister, Fouquet, and since Louis was invited, it was all the more cruel that Fouquet was thrown into prison a few days after the fête for appropriation of public funds. Whether he was guilty or not, we know that the King disapproved of the works of a rival, and inspired by this he began the gardens of Versailles. Many of his shrubs and plants came from Vaux, which to many is still the finest of all the designs of Le Nôtre. It is not the sense of the unexpected, given by the hidden canal that is the secret of its success, but rather the beautiful proportions of the parts leading away from the house.

The genius of Le Nôtre is so stamped on the landscape surrounding Paris, that there is still the impression of a ring of great country palaces encircling

Vaux-le-Vicomte

the capital. Many of these have now been turned into public gardens. Everyone knows of St. Cloud. This is laid out on a steep hillside, the axial line of the gardens terminating on a terrace overlooking Paris. It is impossible to visualize St. Cloud as originally designed, because the palace has been pulled down and the gardens themselves must have been altered. Nevertheless, they form a symphony of green trees and grey stone that is a contrast after the hot streets below on the farther side of the river, and to those who wander from the main paths, the stupendous cascade appears as an added surprise.

   After St. Cloud comes the great terrace at St. Germain. This extends along the brow of a hill for something approaching a mile in length, and is famous for a view over Paris that embraces the circle of hills as well as the city. Just as in England there was at one time a fashion for the planting of avenues, so the making of gigantic terraces seems to have caught the imagination of the Frenchman. Though not equal to St. Germain, the terrace at Meudon is a vast conception, and in the full glory of use must have been a magnificent spectacle. Meudon is another of those gardens where the palace itself has been destroyed, and one cannot help being struck by the number of gardens in France that continue to flourish, while the houses have disappeared within a century or two of completion. Usually it is the reverse. In some ways this is suggestive of their history; the age of the French Renaissance was one in which the enjoyment of the present was paramount. Louis XIV banished all thoughts of time from his surroundings. Architecture and landscape must combine to give the spirit of eternal youth. You will see how Bernini's statue of himself – a fine statue, not over flattering – was removed to the farthest extremity of the Swiss Lake. Clearly this statue expressed something too serious.

The best approach to Versailles is undoubtedly that from Paris, and from the moment you turn into one of the three avenues radiating from the palace, you will realize that here is an architectural conception beyond anything we saw in England. You may say that the wealth that produced Versailles was drawn from an impoverished people, and that it brought about in time the ruin of France. This is true, but few people can withhold admiration for a work of art that must be considered one of the wonders of the modern world. You must ignore the ruthlessness and utter selfishness that made such a building possible, otherwise I would advise you to turn back to Paris.

By this time, if you are wise, you will have reached the Place d'Armes, and the full size begins to be apparent. On either side of the Place d'Armes, and as it were pierced by the three radiating avenues, is the town of Versailles, itself laid out contemporarily with the palace, and containing a number of pleasant squares, houses and gardens of the lesser nobility and ordinary mortals. The emptiness of the Place d'Armes is obvious, for it is a splendid arena for military display. In the middle of the vista, on the first floor overlooking this vast area and the inner courts, is the bedchamber of King Louis. This is the centre, the eye, of all that took place in France and French dominions. How curious it is that one man alone should have been so predominant that his will was law for sixty years.

The garden façade at Versailles is so endless in length that many people think it dull. This would be true were it not that the modelling of the ground in front requires the plain sky-line of the building as a foil. Many people, too, are disappointed in their first walk on the garden terrace. These people are mainly English, and the feeling is probably due to their being unequal to connect such vastness with their previous ideas of a garden. There is that feeling of emptiness which is as apparent here as elsewhere. But as soon as you rise to the spaciousness, and your imagination peoples the gardens with the many thousands for whom it was originally designed, you cannot fail to be impressed by the whole splendid and forlorn beauty. The trees are now in their third or fourth generation, and the sculpture is still young, but the glorious days of frivolity are for ever over.

If you want to explore Versailles fully, you will certainly require more than a day. The vista up the long canal is much farther than at first appears, and if you are enterprising enough to walk, you will find that by the time you have skirted the cross-axial canal, you have walked two or three miles. The twin poplars that appear so slight when seen from the terrace are in reality a group of poplars round a great circle. From here the palace looks disproportionately small, and unknowingly we have stumbled upon one of the great secrets of the grand manner in garden design. It is dear to the heart of many English designers to make a garden appear larger than it really is. This can be done in many ways, but one well-known method is to introduce a kind of false perspective. From the windows of the house, the lines of the garden converge as if in perspective, and this gives the effect of added distance. If you walk about this type of garden, however, you will find

Versailles, the Dragon Fountain and Allée d'Eau

it disappointing, and after a time, mean. Le Nôtre, on the other hand, was dealing with such huge spaces that he deliberately planned the perspective to give the opposite effect. As you walk about Versailles, therefore, the scale of the gardens appears to increase, and you continue to be more and more satisfied by a sense of size. Versailles is full of remarkable studies in landscape design, and the more one knows the garden the more one appreciates the genius of its creator.

There is a well-known plan, made in 1746 by the Abbé Delagrive. To look at this as decoration and not as a garden plan, is to realize how beautiful is the underlying pattern. It is like a design in lace. Yet nothing could be simpler than the idea of cross-vistas and diagonal vistas, within whose fabric are wrought all the curves and rich shapes in which the Frenchman delighted. The human figure, dresses of men and women, and internal decoration, are the three stepping-stones from which we can follow the whole course of French garden detail. Sculpture, parterres, pools and fountains are but echoes of the people of the Court. Old prints especially show this astonishing association between groups of figures and architectural design.

The story of the garden construction is one of conquest over endless difficulties. The site was an old château, and presumably Louis chose this for his palace for sentimental reasons only. The plain is peculiarly arid, and there is no natural water supply. First the whole of the valley was drained to supply water for the fountains and canals; and after a public competition for the solution of this water shortage, a colossal structure was erected on the

Seine, from which water was pumped up under its own power, and taken to Versailles in a great channel. But this too failed, not only because of insufficiency of water, but because although no motive power was required to work the pump, the structure itself was so elaborate and delicate that its upkeep was beyond all bounds. The great aqueduct at Maintenon is almost a more impressive monument to the ambitions of the King than Versailles itself. The plan was to alter the course of the river just by Chartres, and bring the waters all the way to Versailles by canal. Across the valley of Maintenon, a mighty series of arches stands as the last remains of an undertaking never completed. Forty thousand soldiers were working on this scheme, and its non-completion was due to the outbreak of wars.

You soon leave the open terraces at Versailles, and wander away into the woods. If the trees forming the vistas are marshalled into serried ranks, those in the spaces are planted more freely. Within each of these compartments are the most delightful fantasies. None is more lovely than the circular structure of Mansart, whose dainty arches and columns echo the dancers they were designed to encompass. Elsewhere are shady places, spaced here and there with sculpture. Over a hundred of the most famous sculptors of the day worked in the gardens, and the standard of design is consistently brilliant. Leaving the palace farther and farther behind, you appear to be passing into the landscape towards which the vistas have led. But no, for you are upon a wholly new, fascinating world, the world of the Trianons.

Both these palaces were built as a kind of exhaust-valve from the court life in Versailles itself. The Grand Trianon, which supersedes an earlier pavilion originally erected on the site, is clearly a garden structure. One side is separated from the other by a colonnade, and the garden appears to flow through the buildings themselves. Technical garden-planners will appreciate the delightful manner in which the Grand Trianon is attached to the end of the cross-axis of the Grand Canal, and how subtle is the change of angle.

You can imagine how such a delicate personality as that of Marie Antoinette must have been overwhelmed in the full splendour of Versailles. Wherever she looked she beheld the great works of Louis XIV. There must indeed be few cases in history where the personality of a man could continue in so overpowering a way so long after his death. If private life were possible in the palace itself, it was certainly not possible outside the walls; the French garden of this period is ruthless in its lack of intimacy.

This question of intimacy is of absorbing interest in gardens of all ages. In Italy a little area known as a 'giardino secreto' is nearly always found in a large and monumental garden. Hither the owner would come and be detached from his grandiose everyday life. In Austrian gardens we see another idea developed on similar lines, where there is attached to most palaces a little garden called a 'kammergarten'. This would be a small garden extending from one side of the palace into which the owner could walk direct from his private rooms. The 'kammergarten' at Schönbrunn was used up to the time of the death of Franz Josef, which took place in a room

Grand Trianon, Versailles

adjoining. It always seems to me that this human touch in Austrian design, which in other respects followed closely on French theory, makes the difference in the degree to which a garden can be used permanently and domestically. It is indeed similar in idea to the gardens of Bingham's Melcombe, in which the flower garden is a personal garden and the great lawn with the view beyond is impersonal.

So we can watch the emotions of Marie Antoinette and sympathize with her activities in the Petit Trianon. First she seems to have been satisfied with this exquisite little palace, so perfectly proportioned and so set in gardens that it ranks as one of the supreme examples of French architecture. What amusement she must have had from the life within! What fun, for instance, must have been the dining-room table which disappeared underground and returned laden for dinner. Then she feels that even the Petit Trianon is too splendid for everyday living, as indeed it is, and she sets forth on the last stage: the building of the hamlet in the gardens to one side.

The appeal that this little person has made to history is only natural. What could be more terrifying than her background, too vast for comprehension? What more curious contrast than this little hamlet set beside the greatest palace in Christendom?

It seems as though all the world, indeed, had rebelled against the mighty formality which had been stamped upon it; for this hamlet is but a symbol of that wave of Romance that swept over Europe, giving eventual rise in England to the English School of Landscape Gardening. It is no wonder that the Petit Trianon with its gardens is said to be haunted by the gay parties of the past.

It would be as well, now that we have passed through the whole range of French ambitions and the whole range of French emotions that are seen at Versailles, if we were to leave Paris forthwith and go south to our next objective across the Rhine. But no one who is absorbed in French history can fail to walk a few miles to the lovely romantic remains of Marly-le-Roi. Little exists of this gigantic plaything of Louis XIV, laid out by Mansart, except the terracing of the ground, the grouping of the trees, and the view into the blue distance of the Seine. The idea of a central pavilion and detached pavilions standing out at the side is one of the most original in garden architecture. Its wanton extravagance called upon it a worse fate than other gardens, for the Revolution stripped it of everything and left nothing but the undulations of the ground.

Then again, we might take to the air and return on our tracks in order to see at one mighty glance the whole conception of the lay-out of Versailles. We cannot but admire such a great co-ordination of the work of man, and we may realize that the triumph of its co-ordination of landscape is precisely the same as the co-ordination of the valley at Chatsworth, already remarked from a different point of view. From the air you will see all together the great forests and the great remains of the royal and private palaces of the time. On the south side of Paris there will be spread before you as on a plan the palace and gardens of Sceaux. Sceaux is another of those vast conceptions that leave one breathless, and it is to the credit of the people of Paris at the present day that it is being restored and cared for as a public garden.

If you are a person of normal capacity, you will have been so exhausted by this travel through the mighty French gardens round Paris that you would not even wish to come down from your plane (if you were still in the air), in order to see closely the confused, attractive medley that makes up the palace of Fontainebleau; and I think you are right, for from the air you will see how ably has Le Nôtre once more endeavoured to co-ordinate an existing confusion of delightful early buildings by another great scheme of water and canals. The hand of Le Nôtre may lie heavily on the gardens of France, but we must give him his due as the greatest landscape architect in history, and the forerunner of all modern town planning.

Since we are already in the air, let us remain so and continue across the plains of France. From this vantage point we are able to see how different is the pattern of landscape to that of an English countryside. Here in France the open system of agriculture does not call for hedges. The pattern is stiffer and more formal, and, indeed, we can detect an influence of pattern upon the landscape architects. Here and there we see an English park with winding paths and English trees, like a curious oasis. These patches tell the old story of Marie Antoinette; they are little worlds of illusion, escapes from formality. How stocked are the works of Jean Jacques Rousseau with the whole desire of the French idea of escape! Compare this with the English pattern: here we have a more haphazard chequered quilt, outlined by dark hedges. There appears no rhyme or reason for the odd shapes, wandering lanes and haphazard buildings. In England, too, the English trees of the countryside combine with the turf to make a more luxurious carpet, absorbing the garden in their midst.

Nancy is a town which is so beautiful in its central lay-out that we should certainly pay it a visit. But let us leave it as another pattern seen from the air, whence we can appreciate all the more how the twin lines of pollarded limes are more architectural than are the buildings themselves.

The single spire of Strasbourg cathedral is sighted many miles across the plains, and thereafter we cross the Rhine into another world of garden design, so different, so fantastic and so varied in its outlook that before descending upon the city of Karlsruhe we should take stock and see what was the cause of the prolific and extravagant building that makes a tour round Germany so intensely interesting.

Properly speaking, I suppose the crossing of the Rhine should mean a fresh chapter. German and Austrian gardens are totally different in character from the French, but even so, if we survey the Continent of Gardens as a whole we shall see that the three great divisions of garden design across our route are England, France and Italy. By reason of history Germany and Austria are interlocked with France.

It is incredible to think that in the time of which we are speaking, the eighteenth century, Germany was divided into over three hundred free states or cities. Each drew its art from indirect association either with Austria or France. But so indirectly did knowledge flow, and so active and alive were the states themselves, that we find a form of art throughout Germany that is intensely vivid and intensely decadent. One princeling rivalled another in point of splendour. If the palace at Mannheim with its 650 odd yards of façade is the longest in Germany, that at Ludwigsburg with its four hundred rooms has the most accommodation. How such vast courts could be maintained in such small communities is one of those mysteries that is not easily explained.

The recovery of Germany after the terrifying period of the Thirty Years' War must have been extraordinarily rapid. No one, however, felt that they could outshine Versailles, and so the more adventurous hit upon the idea of taking a small theme in garden design and magnifying it to an extent that would by sheer drama capture the interest of the world. Thus it is that to approach Karlsruhe from the air is to see a fantasy carried out on a scale almost beyond belief. The whole plan is radial, and from a centre tower over thirty avenues extend equally to all points of the compass; something over half penetrating through the park, the remainder forming the basis of the town of Karlsruhe. Certainly only one man mattered at Karlsruhe, and if he were not in the centre of the web the design was not really and truly complete.

Karlsruhe is a good preparation for German gardens, for we can now accept other fantasies as more or less rational. But not all are curiosities. Bruchsal lies a few miles north; and apart from having one of the five famous Baroque staircases of Germany, has the remnants of an equally delightful garden forecourt. You should not miss the Chinese rococo pavilion a little way off on the hillside, because it is one of the few examples found on the west side of Germany.

Bruchsal, near Karlsruhe

The course of our route in Germany will now more or less follow the Rhine almost as far as Düsseldorf. In thus going north we are turning from our objective, but that is the licence of the garden hunter. From Düsseldorf, we shall pass across Germany to Potsdam, Dresden, and thence down the east side to Munich.

The old castle of Heidelberg is beautifully situated above the Neckar, with the town huddled below. Here are the remains of one of the most famous of European gardens. Great terraces around the hills and looking down the valley tell of the days when the Castle of Heidelberg was famous as the home of Frederick V of the Palatinate and Elizabeth, daughter of James I of England, in the seventeenth century. Now and then the bridge and castle are illuminated, and there is also a display of fireworks. Hundreds of thousands line the farther banks of the Neckar, and indeed this curious spectacle seems mysteriously to recall the splendours of the past.

From Heidelberg to Schwetzingen is not far in kilometres but they are totally different in landscape and date. You leave behind the tree-clad hills of the Black Forest that at this point lie well away from the Rhine, and proceed over as flat and featureless a plain as you can imagine. The palace of Schwetzingen has thus to form its own landscape without any aid from nature. It vies, too, with the hermitage at Bayreuth as the most decadent of all Renaissance buildings: and how human and charming, therefore, it is. The park is finely laid out and the great central vista and avenues lead away in a manner clearly inspired by Le Nôtre. Schwetzingen is of special interest to garden designers because when the 'English Garden' came to be

The Palace of Schwetzingen

adopted the central formal part was allowed to remain. The combination of the two ideas is most beautifully accomplished, and at no time do you feel the reversal of ideas that has taken place. Among the woods are all sorts of interesting gardens and little buildings. The Indian Mosque may not be happy, but no one could resist the circular Temple of Apollo and the Bath house, with its accompanying series of water gardens.

From Schwetzingen we come to the Rhine and follow its course as far as the confluence with the Maine at Mainz. Nothing remains of the lovely little Favorita overlooking the broad stretch of the two rivers, but you should visit the site in order to see the splendour of the view. As we go down the Rhine the hills now begin to close in on either side. On the east lie the rich vineyards below Wiesbaden whence come the finest of the Rhine wines. Now the hills draw closer still, and we are beginning the voyage that has made the scenery of the Rhine one of the wonders of the world. Here there are no gardens of moment, for it is natural that man's early struggle for existence should be the predominating theme of its landscape. At Coblenz only is there a fine park, to the Elector's palace, and the town is now built on the lines of the old lay-out. So we must pass down the Rhine, stopping only to see the broad lawns and avenues of Bonn, and emerge into the plain that gives rise to the congested city of Cologne.

Bruhl lies a short way from the river, and as the country seat of the Prince Archbishops of Cologne is another example of German design under the influence of Le Nôtre. It is reputed that von Hildebrandt, garden designer of the Belvedere at Vienna, prepared the original design. This is unlikely, because for all its charm Bruhl cannot be compared with the more important work in Vienna.

Now we return to the Rhine and pass through Cologne, that modern industrial city struggling against the heavy odds of a mediaeval plan. As we pass under the Hohenzollern Bridge and see the huge Central Station abutting the cathedral, we cannot help thinking how complicated are the problems man sets himself when building upon history. There are two kinds of towns along the west border of Germany. The one is based on the mediaeval plan and the other on the eighteenth-century plan. While modern development in the former has had to take place round the ramparts, leaving all the necessary open spaces outside and continuing to be as congested as ever in the centre, the other serves naturally as the basis of a modern city. It is composed on the broad, splendid lines of the original Royal palace. These Royal palaces are now public gardens and bring fresh air and spaciousness into the very centre of the town. We should, indeed, be wise to push on as far as Düsseldorf in order to see how beautifully a modern town has been built round the broad, tree-lined central canal of the original park.

In fact, if we are proceeding down the Rhine, we shall be within two or three miles of Düsseldorf, for no garden lover in Germany can afford not to call in at Benrath. This is the most spacious of the Rhine gardens and there is something about the free and delightful use of trees that recalls the English character. Indeed, in Benrath we see something of the grand manner of Bramham Park; as though the English theme of trees has pushed thus far up the Rhine.

If Karlsruhe is the most fantastic garden plan in Germany, the cascade at Wilhelmshöhe, at Cassel, is certainly the most fantastic individual feature. One doubts if anything equivalent to this has been built at any time in the whole world, or is likely to be built in the future. The Landgrave William of Hesse was so absorbed with triumphing over his contemporaries that he shrewdly decided not to emulate any existing garden plan, but rather to take a small feature and magnify it to such a size that all men should behold and wonder.

Cassel lies about the centre of Germany, and a long central axis leads out to the castle of Wilhelmshöhe, two or three miles away. As you approach the castle you see the axis continuing beyond the palace and climbing a range of hills so high as to be often lost in clouds. You pass round the palace, and there before you is the cascade, which rises in giant steps up to a mighty building in the skies. Far away at the top is a copy of the Farnese Hercules leaning on his club. I would not like to say the height of the cascade, but from the lowest pool of the cascade itself to the top of the crown of Hercules cannot be much less than four hundred feet. Eight people can get inside the club.

Just as all Germany near Heidelberg sees the castle illuminations, so all central Germany seems to be drawn to see the cascade play. That was my impression in watching for the water one Sunday afternoon. At the top there is a large reservoir. The water is turned on at four o'clock precisely, and the spectators far below see it gradually tumbling downwards. At twenty minutes past four the last basin is full and the water pours into the last pool. At twenty one minutes past four the reservoir is exhausted and the spectacle comes slowly to an end; there is therefore one supreme minute once a week. Away down the axis, in the meantime, the highest fountain jet in Europe has been roaring, until that, too, becomes exhausted.

When I was describing Wilhelmshöhe to an audience in the English Midlands, a man rose and said he was glad that such neurotic erections had not been made in England. One can, I suppose, agree, but nevertheless this half-finished dream enriches the world more healthily than many a less odd undertaking. In Hanover, which lies farther north, we have a palace and lay-out which would have been approved by our worthy friend. This, of course, was the home of George I, and though we know that the contrast of English with German life at times made the King wish to return, there is something already peculiarly substantial and English in the lay-out. The park may have been planned by a student of Le Nôtre, and is also clearly influenced by Holland. The journey to Hanover is really only repaid, however, when you visit the little garden theatre. This is the most perfect in Germany and I think must have been the largest of its kind. We shall see in Italy a small garden theatre designed to perfection, but here the ballet has taken predominance and the number of wings and dressing rooms, carved in clipped beech, indicate how large were the companies that took part.

The Renaissance garden theatre often seems to have about it a slightly melancholy air. You can so easily conjure up the intense desire for beauty that seems to be partly suppressed in the modern world. The dainty sculptures and fragile hedges at Hanover are not sufficiently robust to exist as part of the life of today.

This cannot be said of our next place of call, the delightful country resort of Sans Souci at Potsdam. In accordance with the taste of Frederick the Great, for whom it was designed, it is a vigorous and distinguished example of eastern German architecture. The original idea was that the palace should be placed in a vineyard, and the architect Knobelsdorff has achieved the effect brilliantly through a series of terraces rising equally one above the other. Vineyards are built into the walls, so that all the fronts are glass, while overhead the grass of the terrace extends to the edge. If you approach from below you will see the little building rising from above the highest terrace, and if you know anything of architecture you will at once realize what has become acknowledged as a classic fault. Frederick insisted that he should be able to walk from his palace straight upon his terrace, without the intervening flight of steps that was customary. He visualized that close association between the rooms of the house and the terraces that would draw the two features closely together. Unfortunately he did not listen to the warnings of Knobelsdorff: if the building were not raised above the terrace, the flights of steps in the foreground would cut off the lower part of the building and give to the building the effect of sinking into the ground.

But it is unkind to criticize a palace which has so much vigour and so much personal charm. It is set in a very large park with another Royal palace, and Potsdam itself is rich enough with lakes and parks to become a kind of German national park. But after all it is Frederick the Great and Sans Souci that have drawn us so close to Berlin.

Sans Souci has given a hint of the Zwinger garden at Dresden, but the only

Sans Souci, Potsdam

real approach to the Zwinger should be by way of the theatrical settings of contemporary German designers. The eighteenth century was the great age of stage design, and so flamboyant were the settings as to make it almost inconceivable that they could have been shown on the stage. Some of the drawings of these stage settings, especially by the brothers Bibiena, have become classics of draughtsmanship. It seems to have been that the architecture of the theatre came to overflow the stage and in the course of time became building itself. The Zwinger is a piece of pure stage setting. So strong and powerful is its character that you cannot fail either to admire or dislike it intensely. There is no doubt that its design is as vigorous as any other, and everyone must admire the attention to detail that makes every

The Zwinger, Dresden

moulding and vase of importance. People it with actors in the costume of
the time and you see how closely allied it is to the stage. It is a kind of echo
of the movement of human beings. And what human beings! It is vulgar,
sensuous, and magnificent. It is Augustus the Strong himself.

We should be well advised to move slowly from Dresden because anything
that we come to see afterwards must be an anti-climax. The long journey
south to Bayreuth will help to break the shock of a visit to the Hermitage,
which lies a few miles outside. You should explore the town first, not only
because of the Wagner theatre but because the Baroque opera house in the
town is perhaps the best example of its kind and becomes a vision of the
world we have just left. The Hermitage was built for the Elector and

Bamberg, Concordia Palace

Electress and can really only appeal on account of the delight of its absolute decadence. The part with which we are concerned is charmingly planned – a semicircle of buildings overlooking a shaped pool gay with fountains. There is a colonnade around the buildings and it is the memory of the Roman Emperors sitting upon these columns of shell-work that seems to stand out as characteristic.

Bamberg lies farther west, and it is probably the mediaeval School of Sculpture that has given the tradition of the excellent quality of later Renaissance details. Certainly you should visit the cathedral, for though there are not many pieces of sculpture in existence they are the finest in Germany and are equal to those at Chartres. There are two gardens in Bamberg, both small and intensely good. The Concordia Palace lies on the banks of the Regnitz and the garden extends along the water's edge. It is a pleasant spot, and now that you can pay a visit without difficulty it is one of those less-known gardens that should not be missed.

High above the river lies the residence of the Prince Archbishop, which forms three sides of an irregular quadrangle. The fourth and widest side is open to the whole of Bamberg, and here a mighty retaining wall drops sheer to the town below. Within this angle is placed what I have always felt to be the most delightful rose garden in the world. There are, I believe, some nineteen thousand plants, and these are arranged in a pattern of box parterre with sculpture arising every now and then. To the Englishman this does not sound attractive, but so beautiful is the sculpture and so well is it proportioned above the rose plants that it seems a perfect combination. As if to give intimacy to this rose garden, pollarded limes follow the ramparts and link together the two ends of the building. Thus the stems of the trees, through which you are

Bamberg, Residenz

still aware of the view, give a slight feeling of enclosure. This little garden is open to the general public; and it seems to me a remarkable German characteristic that there is no protection to the flowers and that no custodian appeared during the hour or two I was taking measurements.

Bamberg is a good preparation for Veitshöcheim, which lies three or four miles north of Würzburg. You should allow for more than a hurried visit, because Veitshöcheim is the most English of all German gardens, and has been described by Sacheverell Sitwell as the most romantically beautiful garden in Europe. It is English in general feeling, because of that curious sympathy between natural planting and formal lines which finds its home in the English landscape. In detail Veitshöcheim is more decidedly French. It is impossible to try to analyse this enchanting garden, so we will lose ourselves among the clipped walks, garden houses, pools and, as I remember it, the beds of dahlias, and take full enjoyment of the moment.

The garden behind the palace at Würzburg is very ingeniously planned, for the terraces follow the lines of mediaeval ramparts. Somehow the great open space in front of the palace and the gigantic size of the palace itself seem to me to dwarf the garden and give an effect of confinement. Nevertheless, there are some good garden features, attractive sculpture, and some of the finest wrought-iron gates in existence. Possibly the most welcoming characteristic of this town garden is its sense of protection, both from the sun, for it is very shady, and from the busy city which lies outside the walls.

So we could find a less desirable place to pause again and review the gardens that we have seen recently and those which we are about to see.

It is a peculiar fact that except for the forceful scenery of the Rhine which we were compelled to penetrate to reach our objectives, the character of the landscape has never greatly intruded itself upon us since we left England. We know that Le Nôtre chose undulating sites in order to impose himself on the landscape and overwhelm natural conditions. In France one feels that French gardens, for all their splendid planning, are the work of one genius. In Germany again we are concerned mainly with variety of architectural design. Now that we are approaching the Alps we begin to wonder if a struggle between man and landscape will take place.

Veitshöcheim, "the most romantically beautiful garden in Europe"

At the outset, it would be unkind not to visit the two great gardens at Munich: Nymphenberg and Schlessheim. Both these palaces are well laid out upon French lines and have, in addition, a certain domestic charm. But for all their beauty they do not seem to me to be so significant in our review of gardens as many a smaller one; therefore we should hasten across the frontier into Austria.

I must confess it is a delicious sensation to come once more under the influence of landscape. Salzburg lies among the Alps, but unlike Innsbruck is not so overwhelmed with colossal mountains on either side as to appear dwarfed. It is a perfect little city crowded upon the banks of the Salzach as it hurries between its twin hills (for they cannot be described as mountains). This little landscape group stands more or less isolated in a plain which leads out on both sides to snow-capped peaks. Home of Mozart and city of music, it is no wonder that its spires and the towers of its churches are themselves rejoicing. On the farther side of the river to the cathedral lie the Mirabelle palace and gardens; the design of these depends more upon surrounding landscape than upon what lies within. The main lines are directed upon Hohensalzburg, the castle which rises sheer above the city. Yet inside the gardens there are a number of delightful places into which one can penetrate and retain a sense of intimacy. The most attractive is the garden theatre; and when, during the festival, there is an operetta, you feel that the gardens are as alive as ever. What does it matter if the acoustics of the theatre make singing almost inaudible, if the spectacle itself is so full of delight?

We have not come to Salzburg, however, to see the Mirabelle gardens and the town, but to visit the little palace and park of Hellbrunn, which lie a few miles to the south. Hellbrunn itself lies in a plain, clinging like Salzburg to its own little mountain. At first sight you might say that here was yet another garden that had to be designed without the aid of nature. This is not the case, because the plains lead away to snow-capped mountains, and it is these peaks that have given the inspiration of design. The details at Hellbrunn are decadent, and we shall be amused by the secret waterworks that spout up

Hellbrunn, near Salzburg

unexpectedly, and still more by the little stage that upon the pressure of a button becomes animated and bursts into a huge volume of sound. These were toys for the loves of Marcus Sitticus the Crafty. But it is not such things that make a visit to Hellbrunn worth while; rather the way in which the architecture echoes the surrounding peaks. I believe it must be the only historical formal garden where larches are happily associated with architecture, for larches themselves are part of mountain landscape and echo the shapes of mountains. That the relation of architectural details to trees and mountains was appreciated at the time is shown by old prints of Hellbrunn, where the artist draws out all these sympathetic qualities.

It may be that the influence of Italy, which we see strongly in the architecture, has made itself also felt in regard to conscious sympathy with landscape.

There are a number of somewhat forlorn gardens throughout Austria which speak of the great days of the Austrian Empire. Vienna was the main bulwark against the Turks in the eighteenth century, and following the raising of the siege in 1683, and the final defeat of the Turks at Zenta in 1697 the building of palaces proceeded vigorously. When we consider how short was the time in which the full flower of Baroque architecture in Austria flourished, we cannot fail to consider it as one of the most prolific of all periods of architecture. Not only, too, in quantity, was building prolific; for the style expresses exuberance. To this period belong the great monasteries. These are famous for their landscape architecture, and there are few finer conceptions of the Church Triumphant than those of Melk, Gottweig, St. Florian and Kremsmunster. Melk is seen from the railway between Linz and Vienna, and even if you are going by the usual train that arrives at Vienna at 9 o'clock in the morning, you should be awake as it passes this glorious building growing from a rock that rises sheer from the Danube.

One always thinks of Salzburg as the city of intimate music, and Vienna that of grand opera. The very shape of the great public buildings, grouped one after another around the Ringstrasse, suggests the rhythm of the waltz. These new buildings were erected by the Emperor Franz Josef in the middle of the last century and occupy the space of a broad circle of open meadows that spread all round the old mediaeval city. The space was kept for military purposes, and building thus took place in a wider ring beyond. Since Vienna lies in a shallow bowl, this outer ring gave the opportunity for a series of sites for palaces that look back over the clustered towers and spires.

The most famous of these palaces are the Liechtenstein, the Schwarzenberg, and the two palaces known as the Upper and Lower Belvedere. Very little is left of the Liechtenstein garden, but old prints show how superb must have been the fantastic little garden structure of the architect, Fischer von Erlach. Nevertheless, what remains of the garden sculpture is some of the finest in Austria.

The Schwarzenberg was also laid out by Fischer von Erlach, and it is worth while entering the gardens at the rear of the palace even though it is only to enjoy the melancholy of decay. Old prints show the garden in the height of its glory, and there is a kind of sad beauty in the tall, untidy trees and the derelict fountains and pools.

On the other hand, the Belvedere garden adjoining is preserved in beautiful condition as public gardens and ranks as one of the supreme pieces of landscape architecture in Europe. The land was acquired by Prince Eugene of Savoy and the two palaces were built for his retirement after his campaigns. The upper palace is more monumental, and was intended for spectacular entertainment. It crowns the rim of the bowl surrounding Vienna, and the garden slopes away in front until it meets the Lower Belvedere. This was used by Prince Eugene more or less as a residence, and we can imagine him in continuous contemplation of the great building at

The Upper Belvedere Palace, Vienna

the head of the garden, the epitome of his military triumphs.

To most people visiting the Belvedere for the first time the most spectacular features are, of course, the maple hedges. These are like walls, being only twelve inches thick and rising to twelve feet in height. They are in perfect condition and form a beautiful continuity of the buildings. Other hedge planting is also interesting, and sculptural details are beautifully designed. You would be wise to approach from the Lower Belvedere in order to obtain the full spectacular effect. From here you will ascend slowly and in time come to see that same view over Vienna above the roof of the Lower Belvedere, for which the terraces were clearly designed.

The garden linking the two buildings gives that curious sensation of a composition of ground and sky that was one of the great attributes of Baroque design. It is, of course, primarily a link between the Upper and Lower Belvedere, and it is interesting to see the firm architectural ties of two wide paths that link together the ends of the buildings. The central axis is not a through way, but is composed of a series of spectacular features. In a garden of this nature a large central path would have given the feeling of dividing the area of ground into two. Also the possibilities of spectacle are less with a single than with a divided path. The modelling of the ground is one of the most outstanding features. The two paths along the boundaries more or less follow the fall of the ground. Thereafter there is a slight change of angle, and within the garden itself there is hollowed out a definite level area. Thus are interlocked the ideas of falling ground and a horizontal floor required by architecture. The level pools draw in the sky and complete the scene.

If the Belvedere is probably the most attractive of Vienna's gardens, the most overwhelming are the gardens of the palace of Schönbrunn. Schönbrunn originally lay a few miles outside Vienna, but the city has

Schönbrunn, the Palace from the Fountain

gradually crept forward and it now forms an accessible public park. A number of monarchs added to the gardens, but they are for ever associated with memories of the Empress Maria Theresa. The first view is terrific. Afterwards you feel that the proportions of the gigantic central space cannot bear analysis.

Away in the woods there are a number of delightful corners. The whole plan is based, like Versailles, on the contrast of open space and woodland excitements. If the Belvedere has the finest maple hedges, Schönbrunn has the finest hornbeam hedges. In avenue after avenue these rise to a height of about forty feet, and their fronts form a sheer and even wall of green. No doubt as you walk about this park you will find these avenues monotonous, but you must remember that they would be traversed in coaches, which themselves would form part of the design. You should, however, walk to the zoo, for here there are not only a good collection of animals, but one of the most charming menageries existing. It is fully circular, with all the cages looking to a central building.

It is perhaps a relief to leave the great park of Schönbrunn and enter the tiny little 'kammergarten' that extends from the west side of the palace. The public were always admitted to the park, and this garden alone was retained as private to the Empress. It is very long and very thin, and its delight depends on its slow change of formality until from the last sequence of shapes you pass into informal forest trees and glades.

Many people will say that, under Jacob Prandauer, Hildebrandt, and Fischer von Erlach, Baroque architecture reached its highest peak in Europe. Certainly it forms a brilliant study, but one cannot help feeling that it grew so quickly and died so quickly that it has not the strength that we find in Italian work. As we leave Vienna and pass over the heights of Semmering, we feel that with the approach to Italy comes something deeper and more profound than is found in any other work of the Renaissance north of the Alps. It is therefore perhaps wise that we should arrive in Italy in the province of the unreal and beautiful city of Venice. For who can take this city seriously?

ITALY

The very flatness of the mainland round Venice gives effect to the isolated houses and palaces and campanili rising from the water's edge. There are some interesting gardens in Venice itself, and although they are small their green foliage is a luxurious change from the everlasting marble, stone, brick and water. But you feel that fair as is the Venice landscape, it is not here that you come to see the Italian garden.

On the mainland there are heavy Palladian villas with remains of equally heavy lay-outs; but Palladio was a town, and not a country architect, and his landscape work is cold and severe. From Venice, therefore, we will not go north but rather west, and travel by boat to Fucina and up the Brenta to Padua. The villas on the Brenta have charm but even the most important, the palace of Stra, has the same unaccountably dull garden. The art of Venice is Seascape. From Padua our way leads south to the first important garden, the Villa Dona Dalle Rose at Valzanzibio. The Euganean hills rise from the flat landscape that stretches from here to Venice and were sufficiently attractive to have induced a Doge of Venice to make amongst them a country home. It is said that the gardens were laid out about fifteen years before the house was built, and we cannot but admire the courage and forethought of such an undertaking.

The garden itself fills a semicircle of the hills. The main axis is thrown from one extremity of the semicircle to another, climbing the hillsides in two cypress avenues. At the foot of one lies a little pink-washed palace, ridiculously small for its huge garden. From the centre of the semicircle a broad water cross-axis leads downhill in descending pools, through a water-gate and out into the plains beyond. This is the basis of the general design. Elsewhere in the garden are various features, such as an island for rabbits, and what is

The garden of the Villa Dona Dalle Rose, Valzanzibio

Fountain, Villa Dona Dalle Rose, Valzanzibio

probably the most perfectly designed and preserved maze in Italy.

We feel at once that here is a harmony of design and natural landscape that is perfectly in accord, a prelude to that association with landscape that is one of the great secrets of Italian garden design.

Leaving the long, shady walks and the sound of falling water which combine to be so refreshing in the hot Italian sun, you should certainly look in at the city of Ferrara, not many miles distant. Over Ferrara looms the great castle of the Estes, and in the palaces and town houses gathered around is that first and early indication of a love for gardens that has made the name of Este famous throughout the world. We should now return upon our tracks and pay a call upon the stucco city of Vicenza. If you can be drawn from the square with Palladio's classic basilica (so beautiful is it), it is worth while leaving the town and walking up a sharp hill to the odd little villa called the Villa Valmarana. There is nothing particularly outstanding in design about this, but it has charm and it was here that John Evelyn paced the length of the garden during the course of his studies in garden design.

The north of Italy is rich in lakes and mountains, and as we cross from east to west we slowly become aware, as of a storm, of the approach of a rising landscape. First, though, the Villa Cuzzano lies a few miles from Verona and gives a hint of that idea of terraced landscape which we shall see by the side of the lakes. Cuzzano is somewhat decadent as to architecture, but the terrace spread before the house has a relationship to the valley that at once calls to mind the great grass lawn at Bingham's Melcombe. Whereas, however, the lawn in the English garden appears to summarize the view of distant green meadows, here it is the shape of elaborate box-parterre that seems to summarize the pattern of furrows that lie on the slopes of the opposite hills. Between cypresses formally placed, this parterre leads on the formality of man until it becomes interlocked with the surrounding landscape.

Just as we have chosen suitable places to pause and consider national characteristics in planning, so we should stop in some place in Italy to consider the design of the Italian garden. There is much to discuss in Cuzzano alone, but Cuzzano is not shady like Valzanzibio, and we should be

Villa Cuzzano, near Verona

wise to press on to a garden designed for contemplation. This means that we cannot wait in that singular garden at Crivelli, not far north of Milan, in which an axis stretches a mile or so across the countryside picking up the villa gardens on the way and in addition a village here and there. No, Crivelli is too energetic, so let us push on to Lake Como, crossing the water to land by the side of the shady, luxurious terrace of the Villa Carlotta. From the terrace you look down upon the lake and the hills rising steeply from it. The lake disappears out of sight at either end, south to Como and north to the Alps.

The lines of our garden are now related to the curves of the landscape, and we realize with a start how the long, horizontal lines of the terrace appear to have arisen from the very surface of the lake. These terrace gardens are water gardens, and just as the long, horizontal lines of ships echo the flatness of the sea, finding their contrast in masts and spars, so these lake gardens echo water, finding their contrast in the sculpture and planting with which they are adorned. How different is this conception to anything we could know in England! It is a sensitiveness to landscape felt by as sensitive a people as any in the history of the world. It is a study in form and shape where the beauty of the flower plays no part, but where all depends upon proportion. Proportion is a mystery given to no man entirely to understand, but a garden shape can give the same sense of pleasure as a well-proportioned room. This, then, is the secret of Italian gardens, and we can see how the emotions have been played upon endlessly.

You may feel, if you are a true Englishman and a patriot, that a garden without flowers is no garden at all. Imagine yourself in the hot Italian sun, living like the Renaissance Italian, and you will then more easily be able to appreciate the qualities of Italian design.

The place of flowers as decoration is taken to a large extent by box-parterre. This is an elaboration of shapes, the interstices being filled up with brightly coloured stones. The effect is similar to a patterned carpet laid on the floor of a room. Many travellers have desired to copy this box-parterre, and in the last century especially it was felt how great would be the improvement if the interstices were filled with flowers. This produced what is known as the carpet bedding of the last century, and gave a false impression to the Englishman of the true Italian parterre. The rich shapes competed with the medley of flowers. It has since been clearly shown how simplicity of idea is essential. Where flowers are the chief decoration, the shape must be kept simple as a foil: such as the long herbaceous border. If, on the other hand, the shape is the first consideration the interest of the material must be all but eliminated. Box-parterre is, in a sense, a reflection of the embroidery on the costume of the period.

There are a number of places on Lake Como that we should certainly visit, though we should beware of doing these gardens in a hurry. Most enchanting of all is the marvellous avenue of cascades of the Villa d'Este, which lead down a gentle slope to pour their waters into the lake. The water steps at Tremezzo rank as a small masterpiece, as does the graceful loggia on the spur that projects into the lake at Balbianello. The Villa Pliniana lies clinging to the rock face on the other side of the lake, and is famous not only for its association with Pliny but because of the cascade that pours through the middle of the house. How much we think of the Romans, who recognized the sound of falling water as a cure for insomnia!

From Como we should pass across broken landscape to Lake Maggiore. Here lies the island named Isola Bella, which to all who come by the Simplon route to Italy is the first sight from the railway of an Italian garden. This rocky little island seems to me to be most attractive when seen from afar in a faint mist. It looks like some fairy ship passing slowly over the calm waters. To land upon the island and walk around cannot but destroy the sense of unreality which the first view inspires.

From Milan the way to Genoa leads past the Certosa, Pavia. The little garden of this monastery is typical of many throughout Italy, and shows clearly how garden design in this country, as in others, grew from the small enclosed area, usually four-square, surrounded with cloisters. There is a fountain in the centre and simple box patterns connect this to the surrounding colonnade. Few more restful places for contemplation could be imagined.

The landscape of Genoa is again something quite different from what we have seen in the past or are likely to see again. The ground rises steeply from the sea, and the great curve of the hills makes a natural harbour. The houses had difficulty in climbing this hillside, but the town has now much character, and terrace upon terrace of houses rises to the sky-line. The 'Street of Palaces' is famous, and the succession of buildings inspired Rubens to spend two years in making an architectural study. Something in their voluptuous strength must have been an inspiration, for we see in his work that same sense of form that is their great characteristic. Today a tunnel has been bored beneath the gardens at the back, so that this street no longer forms the principal link between one part of the town and the other. Many of the gardens climbing the hillsides at the back have disappeared, but here and there is one that tells of the art of the hanging garden. Of these the little Palazzo Podesta is probably the most complete. From the street we climb to the first floor which leads directly on to the garden, and from this latter you climb again to an upper terrace from which viewpoint you behold the whole curve of the bristling, exciting harbour beneath.

To me the garden of the Palazzo Podesta is the most attractive in Genoa. It is not, however, the largest or best known, and any visitor should certainly see the Palazzo Doria. There is a certain harshness about Genoese gardens that is far removed from the luscious terrace of the Villa Cuzzano: perhaps because of the closeness of the rock to the surface and the hardness of the men for whom the gardens were designed. They are far removed, too, from those luxurious gardens of the Riviera farther west, that have been built only for the most wealthy, and planted only with the richest plants.

From Genoa we go south, following the blue waters of the Mediterranean. Pisa lies all white on the muddy Arno, and is a fitting entrance to the valley that is the world's treasure-house of gardens. Pisa, Lucca, Pescia, Pistoia, Prato, and finally Florence form a series of towns that by their very nature are an inspiration for gardens.

Somehow or other the compact, walled city of Lucca gives the impression of spinning round and round. In the seventeenth century the pace increased and it is as though fragments were flung out and never came to rest until they struck the slopes of the hills. Certainly the contrast of mighty walls and crowded city is rarely today seen more clearly than at Lucca. The walls have now been planted with formal lines of trees, which in this age take the place of sentinels. Within the town there are saved a number of open areas, and if you stay the night you will probably be drawn into that hotel made famous by Hilaire Belloc in his *Path to Rome*. When I was here in 1924 with J.C. Shepherd, my companion on these Italian travels, we too were given that

Villa Marlia, Lucca

corner bedroom which appears the vastest in which one has ever slept. The course of this travel to Rome, however, is less direct than that of Belloc, and I think it is only in this bedroom that our ways cross.

The immediate country round Lucca is flat and dull. In the sun it is arid and dusty, but Lucca seems to have an unfair share of rain, and in the rain this area is dismal indeed. Three or four miles north of the city, the plain gives way to the hills, and we strike the first of those white villas that seem to line the range all the way to Florence.

The Villa Bernardini was once approached by a fine avenue, which was cut down during the present century. Like many Italian villas its shape is a simple block with good detail, having a loggia on the north side which overlooks the main part of the garden. This garden leads away from the house to the hills in a very simple rectangle. Its charm lies in the fountain before the loggia which contrasts with the hills; and in the two walks either side of the main axis that penetrate the trees in a series of delightful and varying shapes. But the most memorable feature of the Villa Bernardini is the water-garden that lies to one side of the house. This is at a low level, and is laid out formally with gracious steps, a semicircular pool, and a surrounding wall of shady cypresses.

You must not leave this villa without entering a door in the wall that leads to the 'giardino secreto' that is a favourite feature of the Italian garden, and in its privacy corresponds very closely to the 'kammergarten' that we have met in Vienna. It is a sanctum for the owners of the house, and here they can retire secure in the knowledge that they cannot be found by a casual visitor.

You must assume that despite Lucca's high rainfall you have struck a fine day. A garden like this is laid out for shade and the sound of falling water. Occasionally you have views across the hot, dusty plain, and then it is that you realize why the Italian garden is designed in three materials only – evergreen, stone and water. It is only a few minutes walk to another villa that is not so well proportioned as the Villa Bernardini, but is even more

Villa Marlia, Lucca, "the first theatre garden of Europe"

designed for shade. This is the Villa Buonvisi, and its terraces extending along the slopes of the hills with views towards distant Pisa might easily have made it one of the famous gardens of Tuscany. Other villas call us to investigate what lies behind their white façades and groups of olive trees. But we must press on to what is assuredly the first theatre garden of Europe, the Villa Marlia.

The main garden at Marlia was destroyed during the vogue of the English School of Landscape Gardening, but has since been redesigned by the present owner. The original garden lies to one side, and so enchanting is the first view after proceeding along a drive lined with formal hedges that we must choose this, even though we are standing, as one of these places in which to ruminate. There in front of you is a break in the wall of hedge, and between two garden piers you look across a strip of water to further piers. These again frame a single fountain jet, behind which you see a third pair of piers containing something especially inviting. The vista is on all sides encased with great walls of dark, clipped cypress, which throw deep shadows. How inviting is this view and how curiously we are drawn to enter a world so remote from everyday things! In the first compartment we want to know what happens to the water on either side. Then in the distance we are drawn by the sequence of shapes to see what entrancing mystery lies behind the screen of white foam. So let us enter, and turn abruptly to the left. You will not be disappointed, for here is the most romantic garden feature in all Tuscany.

It seems that while we have ruminated on the theme of expectation (so carefully played upon our emotions by the designer), we must now stop a while to consider another theme of emotion, aroused by this water structure. This belongs to the age of Baroque, and clearly expresses its poetic aspiration. The age finds its greatest exponent in Bernini, who in his Roman fountains seized upon the movement of water and held it in the shapes and forms of his design. It is the architecture of movement, and yet so real and so thoughtful is it that the co-ordination of all the parts retains the static quality of building. Here in this structure you see the rhythm that is set up by the water eddies. It means nothing to us that this structure has no function, and that its surface is decadently covered with ornament associated with water. Our emotions have been aroused by rhythm, and that is enough.

We pass around the pool and enter the second pair of piers to the circular shape which contains the fountain. This we circumnavigate and pass through the third pair of piers, entering garden auditorium and stage. This theatre is very small, but is perfectly designed and perfectly preserved. The auditorium is a semicircle containing clipped boxes for important persons and an open auditorium as stalls. The wings of the stage are in clipped yew in receding planes. There is a prompter's box and conductor's seat and a row of footlights: all in box. Upon the stage are kept three white figures representing Opera (which might be temporarily removed during a performance), and make the garden at all times a furnished place in which to stroll.

Leaving the delicacy and charm of Marlia we must push on to the more splendid and spectacular garden of the Villa Garzoni at Collodi. The broad valley of the Arno seems to have grown a little less in extent and a little less arid. Now we can see the Tuscan landscape of blues and greys. Occasional cypress trees stand out like spires pointing to the sky and clusters of white farmyard buildings with red tiled roofs lie about among the olive trees. From this landscape you can see the gardens rising up a steep hillside and having no apparent relation to the adjoining palace. As you pass along the road to reach the palace a sudden opening reveals the central vista of the garden, and spread before you terrace after terrace rises to the thick ilex-woods. The central vista breaks the woods and continues up a great cascade until at the very top is seen a white figure backed by cypress trees. This breathless view is like a stage setting seen on the rise of the curtain.

Then comes the long climb up the sloping rocks to the palace. This palace is unique, not only for its relationship to the garden (which is designed quite independently, so placed with regard to the windows that it can be seen entirely from the first floor), but also because the central door is the only approach to the village behind. The contouring of the land makes it impossible to construct another road; the palace placed astride seems to hold the whole village from tumbling down the hillside. The head of the garden is approached very informally from the palace, and not until you are at the top of the cascade are you really aware of being within the garden at all. The view from the top is as spectacular as that from below, and when you climb to the terraces and see the gorgeous lower shape contained within a double line of billowing clipped hedges, you realize how rich was the sense of living in such a garden as this.

The road to Florence leads on through a landscape growing still richer, with white villas speckling the hill slopes. How prolific was building of villas round Florence in the times of the Renaissance is indicated not only by those that you see today, but by the stories of how their number ran into thousands. We cannot help comparing this landscape with many a modern scene, where the work of man has destroyed so much of the beauty of nature. This fair valley of the Arno is fair because of man's handiwork.

Soon after Prato, added clusters of white buildings on the hills indicate that Florence is drawing near. In the distance we first see the dome of the cathedral, rising in a curve and drawing together the surrounding hills. Beside it Giotto's campanile acts as a guardian and companion. Farther off rises like a flower the fourteenth century tower of the Palazzo Signoria. Around these buildings, palaces and other buildings now become clear, yellow as though thrown up by the muddy Arno. You may think Florence is noisy with the crack of whips, that it is jostled and unplanned, but few can resist the spell of this fair city.

The Renaissance began in Florence. It was Dante who first broke away from mediaeval doctrine and found the individual soul of man. Thereafter Petrarch and Boccaccio spoke of the beauties of living, of the wonders of landscape and the joy of the world. The tower of the Signoria is like a flower that has opened to meet the sun, and similarly Florence awoke in the fourteenth century to the glories of landscape. You would be well advised to spend some time in Florence looking at the treasures that lie behind the sombre façades, for this will give you some idea of the overwhelming, dynamic force that was occupied in the search for beauty.

It is impossible for us to visit as many gardens as we should like, but the course we will follow is to leave the city by Arcetri and work around in a wide circle from Sesto and Fiesole to Settignano; and come to rest, before our last voyage south to Rome, in the gardens of the Villa Gamberaia. In this way we shall always be aware of the city upon which so many of the villas look.

The Pitti Palace is on the farther side of the river, in point of size the largest palace built in Florence. Rivalry between Luca Pitti and the Strozzis caused the bankruptcy of the former, but he has at least left behind a mighty monument to landscape. Ruskin has described the Pitti as 'Brother heart of the mountain from which it was hewn'; and if we have not been aware of it before, we are now conscious of the change of scale in Italian work to that of England. For a moment we feel puny by the side of these huge and simple buildings. Soon we shall have attuned ourselves to the new standard and come to appreciate the intellectual aspiration that ran so high throughout Italy.

The quarries in the rising ground at the rear of the palace proved an ideal site for the Boboli gardens. You must people the great amphitheatre with memories of the past, the days when all Florence came here to watch a fête; and imagine how during intervals people would flow up the central way and arrange themselves round the terraces at the summit. The tiny little Cavallieri garden is on the highest point of all, upon the ramparts; despite the imposing approach to this little garden, it remains the 'giardino secreto' of the Pitti Palace. From this summit you must descend slowly through ilex ways to the Isolotta, that enchanting oval garden where an island of lemon trees and sculpture and delicious balustrades lies isolated in a water oval.

Far different in every way is the little garden of the Villa Capponi, which enlivens a narrow, steep street in the suburb of Arcetri. High walls conceal what lies within, but few cannot respond to the curves and volutions into

Boboli Gardens, Florence

which the walls break. You walk through the house and upon a broad grass terrace overlooking Florence. To the right is a little parterre garden; to the left appears a parapet wall, from which the ground seems suddenly to drop away. When you approach this wall you see below you two compartments of gardens. You descend into the first by a steep flight of steps and are at once in a world wholly different from that of the upper terrace. Here are all the delights of the small, enclosed garden. Once more in the Villa Capponi we cannot help recalling Bingham's Melcombe; for here, in precisely the same way, are contrasted the themes of open and enclosed.

Michelangelo's villa of Bombicci at Collazzi is too far off and too slight in remains to make a visit possible or desirable, so we will work round the slopes south of Florence and descend to the plain to see the series of rich villas that lie between the city and Sesto. Of these, surely the most delightful must be the Villa Corsi-Salviati. From a hot and dusty road outside you enter through the palace to come upon one of those worlds of fantasy which the Baroque designers loved to create. Sculpture, vases, and flamboyant architecture combine with green parterre and water channels to give a sense of gaiety and delight. It is surprising what a number of features are contained in this simple rectangle, and how curiously decadent, again, is the architecture if examined from the point of view of the purist. The more one sees of gardens the more one enjoys the delightful human failing of decadence in art.

There are a number of Royal villas in this area, notably the Villa Reale at Castello, but these are fifteenth-century gardens, and to many people are not so interesting as those of the following two centuries. They have some

Villa Medici, Fiesole

good detail, the fountain by Tribolo certainly being one of the loveliest in all garden architecture. But we will press on, passing around Florence and threading between gardens that call to us like the sirens of old. The Villa La Pietra is a splendid palace with a new garden laid out to the east; the charm, however, must lie in the little Baroque lemon garden that lies to the north. From La Pietra the way to Fiesole can lead past the old villa of Salviati, which is interesting not only because of the gardens that are laid out for a castellated mediaeval palace, but mainly for the Renaissance sunk garden of parterre and sculpture, upon which you come all of a sudden.

Villa Gamberaia, the Water Garden

Fiesole crowns the hills at this point in a way which compels you to ascend even to the monastery at the highest point. About two-thirds of the way up lies the Villa Medici, built by Michelozzo Michelozzi about 1460 for Cosimo Medici. Here was held the Platonic Academy in which Lorenzo di Medici gathered together the philosophers of the time. The long lines of terraces are carved out of the hill, and it is easy to see how these philosophers paced the terrace in view of the distant city. Because it is an early Italian garden the lines are simple and rectangular, but house and terrace are a fine piece of sculptural modelling, and in few other places is there such a sensation of how the modelling of the natural hill has inspired that of the garden.

Leaving the Villa Medici, we continue our climb and reach the centre of the little town. From here we should descend to a garden on the farther side, for this little estate called La Bardi shows clearly how the Florentine garden has originated from the soil. The house is still more or less a farm, but money has been made, and here and there among the surrounding olive trees are architectural steps and piers that show the earliest beginnings of conventional design. We can judge by this example that there is something similar to the English relationship to the soil in the Tuscan garden, that is unknown to the great gardens of Rome and Paris.

The first view of the Villa Gamberaia immediately creates interest. There is a distinction about the way in which the simple, ivory coloured house sits upon its terrace and is joined to the rising ground by hedges, cypress trees, olive trees, outbuildings, and all the hundred and one features that make a garden. You will not find anything outstandingly spectacular. Nothing that can compare, for instance, with such a view as that at the Villa Cuzzano; nor

Villa Gamberaia, the Long Alley

those inviting walls of the Villa Capponi. But nevertheless you should approach the Villa Gamberaia with respect, because by general consensus of opinion this quiet little group is considered to be the most valuable of all garden documents.

The approach today is between clipped cypress hedges, and leads on to the terrace in front of the house. From here nothing impedes the view from the windows of Florence and the Arno valley. Passing round the house we enter an enclosed water garden, full of life and vitality; and if you are fortunate you will hear what sounds like the note of a powerful organ. This in a moment will be joined by another note in a different key, and later by another. Wondering how so great a volume of sound can materialize from no visible source, you overlook the small frog sitting beside the water. These singing frogs are a revelation to most Englishmen. One, at first of reasonable dimensions, decides to sing and takes a breath that appears to double him in size. He then becomes a bagpipe and produces a note that assuredly no compatriot tenor could sustain, either in volume of sound or length of time.

From here you pass easily into the great alley that is the heart of the garden. This extends from one extremity of the site to the other. One end runs out into the view, the other buries itself in the hills, in a grove of tall cypresses. If you do not want to remain in this alley you pass through an opening in the huge retaining wall that runs along one side. Here is a little garden of steep steps, gnomes and small rock-work that at once recalls so many of the less successful smaller gardens of the present day. From here you pass into a bosco of ilex trees into which the sun can only enter to throw occasional speckles of light upon the broken ground.

Climbing some steps you reach the lemon garden, simply laid out and overlooked by the lemon house. From here you pass again through another bosco and so once more into the alley. You are now led on to the grove of cypresses and come to rest in a garden so deep in cypress shade as to be buried in mystery.

This, briefly, is a descriptive tour of the garden, as it impresses a visitor. We should now analyse how it is that this garden leaves a more profound impression than any we have yet seen. As you sit in the cypress grove you will realize that in a comparatively small space you have visited an extraordinary variety of features. Yet over all there is a sense of repose that can only come through perfect planning and perfect relationship. We know that to take away any of these features would be to harm the garden, and yet how often is it that when we try to plan our own area with a view to variety we produce only restlessness.

First, then, if we study the plan we see how the house and the long alley together form a strong design. The remaining areas more or less fill up the spaces left by these two elements. This sounds simple, but few people realize the great significance of providing a garden with a backbone sufficiently strong to be able to carry a variety of ideas without being thrown out of balance. The best types of gardens are based on an appreciation of human requirements. Let us follow round our course, and this time analyse those areas which on our first visit we enjoyed as we were supposed to do.

First there is a terrace, and here nothing interferes with the distant view. Quite suddenly we pass into the enclosed garden. Here is intimacy, but of an active, everyday type. The long alley is a great contrast, for it is thoughtful, and we shall feel it easy to philosophize while strolling up and down its length. As if to promote this idea, it disappears into a grove of cypresses which themselves promote thoughts away from everyday things. This grove is a form of symbolism and association of ideas that causes the cypress to stand for the Tree of Eternity in a Persian garden, just as the fruit tree stands for the Tree of Life. Overwhelmed by this we then pass into the garden of gnomes, which is a relaxation and means to us what a toy means to a child. The ilex bosco indicates close contact with nature, where the twisted trunks of the trees are a relief from the work of man. How different again is the lemon garden, for here we escape from the intellect and are only concerned with the well-being of the body. The lemon garden is really the kitchen garden, and there is something peculiarly satisfying and English in seeing how the vegetables grow. Thence we pass through another ilex bosco into the alley, and so into that grove of cypresses that cannot fail to invite musing and rumination.

If Florence is the city that gave the first stimulus to landscape, Siena was even earlier in its recognition of the coming of the Renaissance. This little town aboard its hill, crowded within its walls with red brick buildings and campanili, contains some of the loveliest paintings of the early Renaissance. You should certainly visit the small art gallery, for this alone is a perfect example of its kind. As you pass through it and become aware of the Sienese landscapes, you realize that although garden design was late in starting in Siena and that the scope was small, yet the Sienese were as appreciative of their natural surroundings as were the Florentines.

Villa Gori, Siena

The setting of Siena is quite different from that of Florence. It crowns a hill, and other hills seem to tumble about on all sides. It is a heaving, untidy landscape that seems to have broken the crust of the earth and poured forth pink and white lava that cooled and became Siena. From the city a number of villas are seen, and none is more attractive than the Baroque façade of the Villa Gori, with its two long pleached alleys stretching like arms at the side and in front. There is no garden at the Villa Gori except a simple terrace before the house. If you plunge into the tunnel immediately before you, you will arrive at one of those cruel circular structures known as a 'bird-trap'. If, on the other hand, you take the tunnel that leads along the side of the hill you will in time emerge into a garden theatre rivalling that of Marlia. The detachment from humdrum existence of this little theatre is emphasized by its approach, for by the time you have passed through the deep shade dappled only sparsely with light, you will have left the influence of the adjoining city and arrived in a world of illusion. This theatre, with its wings, auditorium, and stage, fills an oval. On the floor of the auditorium there is a charming little design in various patterns. Behind the stage rises a single cypress, which emphasizes by association of ideas the frailty of the stage below.

The greatest architect of Siena was Peruzzi, and one or two gardens as well as a number of villas and town palaces show him to be, perhaps, the most delicate and refined of all Renaissance architects. The Villa Vicobello is very simply laid out, but is notable for its details. Here there is a little garden structure finishing a vista that has become so famous as to be repeated more than once in American gardens. Possibly there is something in American light which would pencil the mouldings with a delicacy that would not be possible in England; but nevertheless you feel that the true home of Peruzzi lies in his Siena landscape, in the Siena light, and among the Sienese.

Another place upon which Peruzzi is said to have worked is the Villa Celsa. This was an old castle, and during the Renaissance a garden was laid out down the hill slopes pointing across the hilly landscape to Siena, just visible some miles away. All the details are again very delicate and there is the distinction of culture in their relation to the mediaeval walls looming behind.

Celsa lies high on the hill, and we have to descend steeply to visit one of the oddest gardens of the Italian Renaissance, the Villa Cetinale. Cetinale itself lies in a fairly level valley, but a range of hills is not far off. The garden consists of nothing more than a single narrow axis that leads straight from the house up a hillside and finishes at a white building at the very summit reputed to be the home of a hermit. Cetinale was built as a summer resort for Flavio Chigi, a nephew of Pope Alexander VII, and clearly he came from sophisticated Rome to enjoy the beauties of natural landscape. Even so, he was unable to leave behind the scholarship and learning of the Imperial city, and for all its single idea the lay-out is as individual as any we are likely to see. The design is based upon the very simple theme of a framed view. At the end of the first stretch of grass that leads away from the house two piers collect the eye and frame the view to the topmost height. But these are no ordinary piers. To many people it is a wonder that the busts of the Roman emperors which have slid down their curves have not slid on to the path below. Others will see in the curves themselves an echo of the curves of the hills above.

So our way leads on to Rome. Every now and then you pass towns like Montepulciano or Pienza crowning the summits of the hills, luring you upwards to inspect the rich treasures that they contain. A diversion should be made by Lake Trasimeno, for here you should go past Perugia to Assisi in order to feel again that glorious sensation of landscape architecture which seems to have come so naturally to the Italians. Besides, the Collegio Rosa lies only a few miles beyond Assisi and short of Spello, and this is certainly

Villa Cetinale, "one of the oddest gardens of the Italian Renaissance"

worth a visit. Here, in a single garden, you can appreciate the beginning and the end of the Renaissance. Oddly enough you must work backwards in time, for your first sight of the garden is across free and easy curves which show the final stages of the Baroque. This part of the garden is said to have been laid out by Piermarini, the architect of La Scala at Milan. On the farther side of the villa a long terrace extends parallel with the slope, which combines with the house to give that same sensation of solidity that we found in the Villa Medici at Fiesole. We can, then, see how the Renaissance began with an early sculptural solidity and passed some four hundred years later into a lightness and frivolity that lay on the surface only.

   When we come to Viterbo we at last begin to feel within the orbit of Rome, for near here is one of those great country seats that tell of the influence and splendour of the Vatican. Many of those villas which we shall find

Villa Lante, Bagnaia

plentifully at Frascati are so robust as to appear coarse after the work of Siena or Florence. This is not the case with the Villa Lante, Bagnaia, which lies a few miles from Viterbo. If we can say that the Villa Gamberaia is the most human of all gardens, we can say equally that the Villa Lante is the most imaginative.

The site is a gently sloping, wooded hillside, leading direct to the town of Bagnaia. Water was plentiful and came trickling downwards through the trees. This theme of landscape was not to be altered, but was to be an inspiration of a formal design suitable for the enjoyment of man. There are two villas, not one, and they are symmetrically arranged with the garden flowing between. It is as though more importance has been given to the idea of a garden than to the idea of a house. The garden descends from the woods with a centre line of water which passes through different fountains and rills, and on the way is turned into innumerable patterns. As it approaches the twin houses it becomes more tamed and formal; and culminates in a square, patterned water-garden, from the centre of which rises a group by Giovanni da Bologna. There is that easy approach from the mystery of nature to the calm formality of architecture that is the aim of all persons seeking intimate communion with their natural surroundings.

Quite another matter is the mighty Villa Farnese, which dominates the central road of Caprarola like a great mediaeval castle. This, too, was built by Vignola, and no doubt there was something in the powerful, pentagonal mass that proved even too much for Cardinal Alessandro Farnese. Formal gardens extend from two sides of the pentagon, but you do not feel that they are homogeneous with the building. You wander away into the woods at the back and after a short time come upon that queer, fantastic lay-out that can only be described as the most monumental of all 'giardini secreti'. Your first view is of two huge stone sentinel boxes, framing a vista the centre of which is occupied by a cascade of fishes biting their tails all the way down. The eye runs up this sparkling centre, past some water giants, and so to the

Villa Lante, the Water Garden

little pavilion and loggia that crowns the summit. As you walk up beside the rill you enjoy the delicious chuckling noise that water makes as it falls from shell to shell. You soon reach an oval shape and ascend a curving ramp divided by the giants. You are now on the lower terrace in front of the pavilion, whose loggia on the first floor corresponds to the level of the ground at the back.

This garden is laid out in box-parterre, and its rectangular shape is defined by the oddest caryatides imaginable. It is said that Michelangelo was responsible for some of the sculpture, which is as fine as any in Italy. Besides, these caryatides are human enough to appeal even to Englishmen. They are all different, and are so obviously enjoying conversation the one with the other upon matters of topical interest that you feel immediately at home. The architect will appreciate that they give not only ornament to the garden but that same sense of enclosure that was given by the stems of the pollarded limes in the Archbishop's palace at Bamberg. On three sides lie glimpses of the distant view, now divided into a series of constantly changing pictures.

We pass through this garden and ascend a ramp, with more dolphins in the water, to the upper terrace at the rear. We are now beside the most perfectly proportioned loggia in the country. It seems a strange thing in human nature that this little pavilion and garden were built on such a colossal theme, when all they were meant to do was to give relief from the splendours of the villa adjoining.

It almost seems, as we approach the Roman campagna, that the scale of the countryside grows grander; as if it, too, were conscious of the history of the Eternal city. One wonders how most dramatically to break through that circle of hills that stretch like distant guardians around Rome. It is certainly not surprising that as soon as the country was safe people left Rome during the height of the summer and took up their residence on these surrounding hills. Rome itself is built on seven hills, but they are too modest to give more than undulations; all that appears from afar is a slight disturbance in the placid sea of the campagna. One disturbance a little more emphatic than the rest lies in the dome of St. Peter's, which floats like a bubble on the surface.

But we have not yet come upon this view, for we are still threading our way up the sinuous road at the back of Tivoli. How often must the Roman legions have marched through these hills, along roads that extended over the whole of Italy and Europe, as far north as Hadrian's wall in England! You are bound to feel a reverence in approaching a city that in classic days was Mistress of the World, and you cannot help feeling a certain reverence, too, for the great villas we are going to visit, which tell of the line of Popes stretching unbroken back to St. Peter. If you have cause to doubt the wisdom of the Church in enjoying so full a luxury of living, you will have the same sensations as when we turned and first saw the great Avenue to Versailles. But you should put these doubts to rest, for otherwise they will spoil your enjoyment of what are some of the grandest works of art and landscape.

You hear the falls of Tivoli before they are actually seen, and like the Roman Emperor of old who came to find sleep within the sound of the water, you will want to sit down and rest from the heat. There, opposite, is the Temple of Vesta, standing on a rock above the white falls that disappear into the depths. It is some of this water that has helped to make the Villa d'Este the most dramatic and spectacular of all gardens; indeed, if we drew up a list of the seven wonders of the gardening world, this villa might well rank as the first.

The gardens are built down an abrupt hillside and come to rest on fairly level ground. On the topmost terrace, with your back to the Villa, the ground extends round to the right at the same high level. On the left it falls away in mighty retaining walls and there you will have your first view of the Roman Campagna. Yet it is doubtful whether this is the finest view and we should do well to wait until we come to the great terrace gardens at Frascati before giving the campagna full contemplation. So let us turn back and explore this gigantic water-garden.

If the sun is hot outside, and traffic crowded on the roads, you will already have become aware of a vast soothing organ of sound. This is water falling in a hundred different ways, producing, as you walk from place to place, an ever-changing variety of chords. There is the Terrace of a Hundred Fountains, each consisting of a jet splashing into a water trough. There is a single jet that rises in the central path descending the hillside; and there is, above all, the huge cascade that is made from a river diverted to flow through the gardens. This tumbling, seething mass of water crashes into its own basin and is thereafter led away into a series of quiet, reflecting pools towards the campagna. The peace of these immobile pools is beyond belief. It is they which give the vitality and energy and sense of activity to the whole

Villa d'Este, Tivoli, "the most dramatic and spectacular of all gardens"

of the rest of the garden. Everywhere is deep shade, and as we pass to the tallest group of cypresses in Italy we should do well to turn and look at that stupendous view, of terrace rising upon terrace, steps upon steps, and structure upon structure that leads up and up until it meets the villa at the top.

From the viewpoint at Este we can see the white villas of Frascati sparkling in the sun. There is generally a haze of heat lying over the campagna, and this gives a slight touch of added blue to the thinly green fields and grey olive trees. Even though Hadrian's Villa calls us into the campagna at the foot of Tivoli we should be wise to work an imaginary path round the hills and approach Frascati without entering the hot campagna.

Frascati is a glorious community of gardens. The town itself is certainly important, but you do not feel that it matters. Possibly the imposing position of the Villa Aldobrandini gives the impression that this villa is the central force of a community, on one side of which lies the town, while all around are gardens. You are certain to visit first the Villa Aldobrandini (and indeed I know of few more attractive approaches to Frascati than to come over the hills from Tusculum and descend through the wooded slopes. How it is that you find yourself in the gardens of the Villa Aldobrandini I do not know, but you are at the head of the cascade that leads steeply down the hill to the rear of the villa). If you enter the villa itself, and climb to the topmost loggia which looks back upon the hillside, you will see how cleverly the cascade has been planned to give the illusion of an almost vertical fall of water. This is one of those exercises in the arts of perspective in which the Italians have always delighted.

From here we should visit the Villa Lancelotti which lies adjoining. Two lengths of pollarded trees extend symmetrically from the villa and finish by a pool and garden structure. The front views of the villa look out towards Rome (in this case over the roofs of Frascati), while the garden buries itself, as it were, in the hillside at the rear. This simple rectangle is filled with an elaborate box parterre, which lies like a carpet and gives to the whole garden the air of an extra salon to the house. We can judge particularly well how the Italian garden with its permanent materials is so closely akin to architecture. Only the evergreens put on a new dress in spring to indicate the passing of the seasons.

All people love the Villa Falconieri, for who could resist that lovely reflecting pool which doubles the tall cypresses around the edge and catches the clear blue of the Italian sky? Yet another villa that we should see on this side of Frascati is the Villa Borghese. There is a fine semicircular staircase at the rear, but one's chief delight must lie in the terrace garden. This is more intimate than many at Frascati, and it is possible to escape from the view in the group of trees that surround the central fountain.

These estates abut one another and are joined together in many instances by shady ilex alleys. Our way leads up a slight incline and is stopped by the garden gate of the Villa Mondragone. This splendid group of buildings, perhaps the greatest of all those at Frascati, contains the least of Frascati gardens. Within the building there are some enclosed gardens, but our object is the great terrace that lies in front of the villa and rises steeply and imperiously above the campagna. I cannot decide whether to let this sky garden be the end of our travels, or whether we should choose the broad terrace of the Villa Torlonia. It has become clear as we have drawn near our destination that we shall not enter the Imperial city but will see it like an enchanted city in the distance.

There is a single fountain on the terrace of Mondragone, and beyond this there is nothing between the palace and the distance. The sky is reflected in the water of the fountain, and so grand is the scale of the architecture

Mondragone, Frascati

that you feel once more what we have felt from time to time, that here is that co-ordination of landscape and sky that is the ultimate aim of garden design. This, too, was designed by Vignola.

So we will leave Mondragone to walk back through the shady alleys into the square in front of Aldobrandini and enter the last garden of our travels.

The first impression of the Villa Torlonia is one of lines of great terraces running parallel to the hillside, backed by a mighty wall of ilex. Huge ramps and stairs connect one terrace with another and tell of the days when thousands would come from Rome for the enjoyment of the view. We, too, might well rest on this hillside and contemplate our last view of the campagna. If you have left things late the sun will have gone down, the light turned to a blue-grey, and away across the flat campagna the long lines of ruined aqueducts will become less marked. Here and there on the Alban hills lights will begin to appear like pale stars in the sky. Far away in the distance the city will become gradually less defined, and soon disappear.

We might well leave this as our last memory, but I think it is a view too large for the Englishman to absorb; so let us turn as the wise Italian had intended us to do, and walk among the dark alleys in the ilex wood. Here the sound of roaring water will draw us inevitably to that cascade that surpasses all others for dignity and grandeur. It is within the sound of these waters that I think we might stop awhile and rest.

INDEX